Profit from
Effective Communication

PICSIE BOOKS
P.O. Box 786340
Sandton 2146
Tel (011) 442-8175

NEAL DUBREY

Profit from Effective Communication

1990
JUTA & CO, LTD

First published in 1990

Copyright © Juta & Co, Ltd
PO Box 14373, Kenwyn 7790

ISBN 0 7021 2376 5

Printed and bound by Chelsea Press, Hillstar Road, Wetton 7764.

'The Problem with so many people is that they cannot communicate. They seem unable to put their thoughts into words. Do you agree?'

'Grunt.'

Foreword

By Professor Danie Theron

At present it seems that an almost universal enthusiasm exists in the pursuit of excellence in the conduct of human affairs and human endeavour. Reading the numerous recent publications on the management of administrative, industrial, commercial, professional, institutional and even domestic activities, it is clear that there is a renewed imperative to do something to achieve superior performance—it has even been described by some as a revolution in the achievement and sustaining of success.

A key component in this pursuit of excellence is of course communication, and at a time when the means of communication are proliferating at a bewildering rate it is essential that all the basic principles of effective communication should be clearly understood by those aspiring to levels of leadership.

In the Department of Architecture at the University of Port Elizabeth we are privileged to have a lecturer of the calibre and enthusiasm of Neal DuBrey. Over the years he has developed his ideas in his course on the theory of communication. These ideas, on how to clarify one's own views of a specific area of experience, and on how to communicate rationally, passionately and effectively in order to persuade, and to generate enthusiasm in the 'change business', are now available in this publication.

I recommend this book strongly to anybody in search of excellence.

Port Elizabeth 1989

Contents

Introduction

What business are you involved in? Or what profession or trade?

No matter what your field of activity, whether you are starting out or well established, this book is written for you. It is a real gold mine of practical, helpful advice.

It will help you to develop your personal communication skills—to form thoughts into words—to listen effectively—to write clearly—and to benefit from the use of sound argument and persuasion.

Learn from it and you will profit, both materially and in terms of your advancement and self-fulfilment.

More—there is a valuable bonus. Better communication will lead to a better social life. You will be able to talk more easily to people, in groups or one to one. So you stand to gain in personal riches too.

The course on which this book is based has been successfully used at the University of Port Elizabeth for many years and forms the basis of lectures and seminars given to Commerce and Industry. It is founded on a wealth of practical experience and application.

It is all proven. It all works.

All you have to do is to read the text, practise the simple exercises and use what you have learned.

You can only gain.

1

Call for a change

■ **Nothing changes on its own. You have to make it change. As an innovator, as a leader, you have to call upon others to make those changes which you require.**

■ **Your instructions to them must be precise. Or nothing will happen or, worse, there can be a disaster. So you have to know how to *communicate*.**

'We cannot live alone, inside of our heads, in the islands of our minds'.

But we can of course, and many people do. They exist, as mental hermits, they are isolated. And they miss so much.

To live our lives to the full, to succeed, to make things work, to share in all the excitement of the human carnival, we have to *participate*. We have to free our thoughts, send them winging out, and we do this by talking.

Just as important, we have to gather back the thoughts of others. We have to listen, too.

This free flow of ideas, of knowledge, of emotions, mind to mind, is human *communication*. Which is what this book is all about.

This course works. Here are skills which will help *you* to communicate, which will profit *you* in your chosen profession, or in your business, and socially. These are the proven practical skills of *EFFECTIVE COMMUNICATION*.

Headlines and benefits

Sit back for a moment. Think back on what you have read. You have been given two basic messages:

First: This book concerns communication—a **HEADLINE** (what this book is about).
Second: This book teaches effective communication—the **BENEFIT** (which you stand to gain).

We are used to headlines, we see them in our newspapers every day. We first encountered headlines at a very early age.

As small children, about to be read a story, we used to ask, 'What's it about?' We wanted to know if the subject would interest us. If the story would be worth being good.

And we still want to know, 'What's it about?' On any offer, any communication, such as this book, we ask ourselves, 'What's it going to be about?' and 'How can that benefit me?'

For, let us openly accept the fact, we are all basically selfish, all out for Number One.

'Tell me what I stand to gain and I'll pay attention.'
So, to gain the attention of others whenever we have to speak from a platform or to a small informal group or even in everyday conversation, we should start off with a **HEADLINE**:

'What I am going to talk about.'

Followed by the **BENEFIT**:

'What you will gain by listening.'

(The full technique for assembling your effective 'Spoken Communication' comes in Chapter 3. There we cover speaking to audiences large and small.)

You may seldom have to speak from a platform to a large audience—all those rows of eyes—but in very many normal business and social situations you will certainly be called upon to 'say a few words' to a smaller group.

Also, you will be involved in selling.

> 'No, no, no. I'm not in sales. I'm not a selling sort of person. That's not me.'

All of us have to sell, although perhaps not across a counter or as a 'rep'. And not goods or services. We have to sell *ourselves*. We have to sell the 'who' and 'what' we are, our abilities . . . We have to sell ourselves continually. Or be ignored.

This course will help you in selling. If you are poor at selling it will make you good. If you are already good at selling it will make you great.

The Audience of One

Do not assume that a 'communication' has to be to a group. Very often you will want to pass your ideas to an audience of only one person. But a very important person!

- The Big Boss, across his desk.

- Your Very Special Love.

When you speak to either of these, the clear expression of your thoughts can be vital.

> 'I want to speak to you about the low figures this month. I can explain it all.'

> 'Let's talk about us. I can make you very happy.'

Do you see the 'Headline' and the 'Benefit'?
All common-sense, isn't it?

I teach common-sense. The other day a lady came to me during a break in a seminar and said: 'You know, you don't talk about

anything really new or far out. You merely point out the inade-
quacies of our usual day-to-day communication, and then you show
us the common-sense ways to improve.'

I took this as a compliment. I do not try to theorise or innovate.
I merely want to demonstrate what works.

Demonstration—This Course Works

One day on campus a student came to me in great excitement.

'Hey!' he said. 'Your course on communication works.'

'And how did you find out?'

'Well, this morning I was stopped by a cop. He claimed that I
had jumped a stop street. But I remembered what you had taught
us, especially the bit about how to "Persuade people your way". So
I just did what you said. And he let me off.'

'I'm disappointed', I said.

'Why? Because I used your techniques on a cop?'

'No, no. You are free to use my techniques on anybody. Any
time, any place. That is what they are for. I am disappointed
because you *did not hear*. In my very first lecture I told you that I
would be teaching you skills that work. You listened, but you did
not believe until you were forced to apply. You should have already
proved to yourself, long ago, that this course works. You should
have been using each technique as soon as you learned it. They are
all practical. They all apply every day. They are yours to be used.'

> (There will be more on listening later. And plenty on how to
> persuade. This will help you to be able to argue the point
> with a traffic cop should the need arise, and in many other
> situations too.)

■ **There is nothing more frustrating than knowing you are
right, while lacking the skill to convince.**

After each chapter in this book there are exercises for you
to practise. They are based on the practical periods which

are an essential part of the university course. Do not think, if you have long been out in the real world, that such exercises hold no value for you, that you are beyond them. Or that exercises alone will be enough. You will have to get out there, start using all that you learn, at every opportunity.

You have to practise all that you learn. Only in this way will you gain full benefit. This is not a book to be laid aside with a 'Too true, that makes sense'. This is a 'Manual of Effective Communication Techniques'. To be read, understood, and *used.*

You can start right now. Speak to people more. Move out of the confines of your mind. Talk. Not only to friends and colleagues. Talk to strangers. Try this. Start today.

Speak up to be noticed

I once went through a Silent Period.
I had noticed in the movies that the hero stood aside with jaw set firm, aloof and silent.

And the heroine went flippity-flip towards him.
I tried this.
I stood aside with jaw set firm and was aloof and very silent.

Absolutely nothing happened . . .

■ **If you do not speak up for yourself you are ignored. Nobody notices that you are around.**

I have a friend who talks to absolutely everybody. He talks to people in queues, in shops, in lifts, everywhere. And all strangers. Yak, yak, yak.

I used to be embarrassed by all his chatter. Until I realised that all these people he talks to actually *enjoy* the experience. They smile, they preen, they walk tall.

All from ordinary conversation.

So please talk to more people!

(And never forget that your employees are people too.)

Apart from the pleasure you give, the sunshine you spread, you will be doing yourself a favour. You will be practising putting your thoughts into words.

It will be pretty much everyday chatter, of course, small talk, but no harm in that.

It is *talking* and *listening* you are practising, not erudite content.

WARNING!

There is one situation in which this talking to strangers does not work.

> Some years ago I was travelling, among businessmen all in dark suits, in a British Rail first-class carriage. Nobody spoke, of course. We had not been introduced. We all sat silent, reading our copies of *The Times*. I had finished most of mine. I was down to the 'In memoriam' column.
>
> 'HAROLD, King of England. Died defending the Realm against the Norman Invader. Hastings, 1066.'
>
> I nudged the elbow of the silent figure seated beside me. 'Hey, see this?'
>
> He read through it slowly. 'So?' he said.
>
> Which is a lengthy conversation for a British Rail first-class carriage.

Here in South Africa you should encounter few such difficulties. We all like a chance to chat, hey!

Call for a change!

Now on to more serious types of talk. To a group, in committee, or across a desk.

In situations where you need to call for change.

■ **Whatever business you may be in, you are in the change business.**

■ **Each time you speak you should be calling for some sort of change.**

If you do not, nothing will happen, because you have not asked for it. You will have accomplished nothing and it will be your own fault,

But if, each time you speak, and on account of what you say and how you say it, and because you **ask**, the world changes a bit in your direction, if only a tiny bit, you are winning!

A man stands up at a committee meeting and he waffles. On and on and on . . .

'What's he on about?'

'What does he *want*?'

You will be familiar with this situation. It often happens at committee meetings. Where there is so much talk, but so few good suggestions, on what exactly is to be done.

A call for change is a *proposal.*

We can develop further on the classical proposal, the start of which we have already noted:

'Let's talk about us   (Headline)

I can make you very happy.'   (Benefit)

To which can be added:

'Will you marry me?' (Proposal for **CHANGE**)

And quite a significant change, at that!

There are three broad types of change which you can call for:

• Change in *level of knowledge*

• Change in *attitude*

• Change in *behaviour*

Which happen to be the accepted basics of motivation theory.

An example, in a selling situation:

1. The salesperson first proposes a change in the level of knowledge of the customer.

    'Let me tell you what this product will do.'

2. Followed by a request for a change in attitude, usually from negative to positive.

    'Isn't this just what you need?'

3. With, finally, the call for a change in behaviour, from doing nothing to doing something, which is the call for action.

    'Sign here.'

In real-life situations these three stages are seldom so clear-cut, nor do they necessarily have to follow in the same sequence. But it is as good a sequence as any, and logical.

PROFIT FROM YOUR PROMOTION OF CHANGE

First, change level of knowledge.
(Which is easy, there is seldom resistance.)

Second, change attitude.
(More difficult, people are so conservative.)

Third, change course of behaviour (action).
(Not easy, especially if it involves the spending of money.)

Of course, you do not need to call for all three changes every time. You can instruct, or change attitude, without actually having to ask anybody actually to *do* anything.

But it is always a good idea, when you are going to call for action, to use the full sequence.

Inform first, encourage the thinking to move your way, then call for a shift in behaviour towards making things happen. Remember that it is your call for action that initiates the change, that gets things moving.

Any change you call for, of whatever type, must fulfil three essential conditions:
1. It must benefit you.
    (Otherwise why ask for it? Yet people continue to demand changes that not only would not benefit them but would not benefit anybody. They ask to assert their 'authority'.)
2. It must benefit your audience.
    (Otherwise, being selfish, why should they change?)
3. **IT MUST BE POSSIBLE!**—by not being possible, many appeals for change are doomed to failure.

A great deal of time is wasted by a great many people calling for great quantities of changes which are just not possible!

Usually, it is actions that are not possible. We do not mind learning something new, or changing an attitude, even, but when we are asked to *do* something. Who? Me?

And in selling there is the sale that fails because the customer has no money. He would like to buy, he really would. Only he can't.

I once met a helicopter salesman (not many helicopter salesmen about) who gave an interesting example of 'not possible' attempted selling. As you know, much selling is initiated by setting out the benefits. But you do not need to spell out the benefits of owning a helicopter. It is the ultimate status symbol. Imagine a helicopter, standing out there all shiny on your own front lawn. It would turn all the neighbours green with envy, greener than the grass.

So this helicopter salesman has no difficulty in finding customers who would 'like a helicopter' and who appreciate the benefits but who would waste his time.

He has to work very hard to find those very few, usually among the larger corporations, to whom a sale is possible. The few who can afford to pay.

■ **The call for a change which may be desirable, but is not possible, I define as 'preaching a sermon'.**

Such a sermon puts forward a proposal which is gladly accepted, but which it is not practical to carry out.

Example:

On a Sunday morning the preacher says, 'Love thy neighbour.'

His congregation happily accepts this. 'Love thy neighbour.' It is a good attitude. The proper way to go.

But sometimes difficult to put into practice . . . For what is neighbour doing, that very same afternoon? Neighbour is having a braai, that is what neighbour is doing, and playing loud music too. While our member of the congregation is trying to snooze.

So what does our member of the congregation do? He shouts over the fence, 'Turn that bloody racket down!'

He does accept the principle of 'Love thy neighbour'. He really does. But it is not so easy to carry out.

Not all sermons, given in church, I hasten to add, call for impossible actions.

Nor are all 'sermons', by my definition, given from a pulpit.

> He: 'Chuck your job. Come with me to Mauritius.'
> A 'sermon'. She would love to go, she really would. But it is not possible. Her husband wouldn't like it.

There are very many worthy people, making very many worthy appeals, from platforms and across desks, up and down the country, delivering 'sermons' each and every day.

Their audiences agree with all that is said. Every word. Their attitudes are changed.

Yet the members of these audiences do not act upon whatever it is that they are being urged to do. They might agree. They might even *want* to act. But the action called for is just too *difficult* for them to carry out. So they search around for a good excuse. And then they do nothing.

Happens quite often in business . . .

Example of a 'sermon' type of appeal. In written form this time for we must remember that communications can be written as well as spoken. (More on effective written communications later.)

It is a slip of paper dropped into your post box at home. The message is simple, 'Support your local hardware store'.

You nod in agreement as you read. This is true, you know. The poor old guy at the hardware store has all that expert knowledge, and he's always so obliging, so willing to help. Yet he seems to be desperate for business.

OK? Accepted in principle? Attitude changed? Right on. Until next week we break a door handle, or lose a kitchen knife, or need a bag of nails. Then off we go to the nearest discount operation, which has all the same goods as the kind old man full of advice at the hardware store, only much cheaper.

■ **People are selfish,**
  they watch their money,
  they are lazy.

■ **And they tend to take the easiest way out.**

Of course, it *is* possible to persuade people to do something that is not so easy for them, but you will have to be very persuasive and you will have to offer real benefits. 'Save time and money. Buy from the expert.' Our hardware man would have gone further with this type of approach, which is an appeal for a change which becomes possible because it does offer some tangible benefits. It is now less of a sermon, more of a proposal.

Now what have I been offering to you, in asking you to accept these first principles of communication? In asking you to use 'Headlines' and 'Benefits', in asking you to talk more freely, in asking you always to call for change?

Is my appeal a proposal, or a sermon?

It is a proposal, of course. It is entirely practical, and possible, for you to change. You can start making use of the first basic communication skills immediately.

And gain more success for yourself, from right now.

Talking to a Group

Much of the training in this course is directed towards talking to an audience.

Which is 'Public Speaking'. Although this is much more than a course in Public Speaking. The scope ranges far wider.

It is a fact that many skills of communication can be more easily taught, and more easily learned, by working on 'talking to a group'. These skills lead to greater confidence, clearer thinking, better listening, and more. Proficiencies which can be of great general advantage to you.

You will have noticed that those who are fluent when talking to a group also shine in conversation. This is no coincidence. They are using the same basic skills, in wider application.

Or you may aspire to more formal speaking, to large audiences, from a platform. You will need exactly the same basic proficiencies.

So . . . that is why there will be some concentration on 'talking to a group'.

■ **The required skills are easy to understand.**
■ **They can be widely used.**

Talks, Lectures and Speeches

Some confusion. What are the differences, if any? We should clarify before we proceed. It is important.

A Talk is 'about something'.

'Mrs Mange will talk to us about hydrangeas.' All quite interesting, no doubt, and you may learn something (change your level of knowledge) but does it really *matter*?

Talks are inclined to be too specialised and to go on for too long. There is a real danger of a pet hobby-horse being ridden off at a gallop . . .

> Kind old museum guide to little girl, after he has given his talk on penguins: 'Well, and how did you enjoy that, my dear?'
>
> 'It told me more about penguins than I wanted to know.'

Most talks tell us more than we want to know.

• There is no call for change of attitude in a talk.

• There is no call for action.

A Lecture is a talk on a somewhat higher plane. It also gives a series of facts, again seeking to change your level of knowledge, but more usefully. (If you feel that you should be taking notes for future reference, then it could be a lecture.) A lecture may also offer some new and original thought, a touch of philosophy, even criticism and review. Although this is rare.

- A lecture does call for a worthwhile change in level of knowledge.

- A lecture may call for a change in your attitude.
  If you do not agree with what is being said, you may debate with the lecturer at question time. If you do agree with what is being said, you are not encouraged to scream for some action on the matter. A lecture is all rather dignified.

- A lecture does not call for behavioural change.

A Speech, that is a good solid speech, and there are very few good solid speeches about, changes level of knowledge, revises attitude, and does call for action.

Also, a speech is of the moment. It deals with *now*.

■ **A speech should say exactly what should be said, at this moment in time. What is in everybody's mind. What they seek a mouthpiece to express.**

■ **When the time for a speech has gone, even a good speech loses its meaning.**

Abraham Lincoln said in his address at Gettysburg, 'The world will little note nor long remember what we say here today.'
This has become one of his best-known messages. It was quite correct at the time. It is quite wrong now.

A Wedding Speech is also 'of the moment'. All that needs to be said for a wedding speech is how pretty the new bride is and how we all agree how lucky the groom is and 'Thank you Auntie Lena for coming up from Joubertina'. That, and a call for a couple of toasts, is all that is expected. There need be no lasting message.

The 'On Your Retirement' Speech. Dear old Enid, she has worked in the mailroom for twenty two years. In that time she has lifted innumerable items of stationery, for the use of her children, and later of her grandchildren, and she has whipped all her personal mail through the office franking machine.

This is not the occasion to mention this. All you need to say today is, 'Good old Enid. We all join in wishing you a happy retirement. Please accept this ball-point pen.' Somebody should have brought up the other matter twenty-two years ago.

The point here is not to show the typical content of these special occasion speeches. The point is to emphasise that a good and effective speech must deal with matters that are in the minds of the members of the particular audience *at that moment.*

- A speech should not drag up from the past that which is best forgotten.

- A speech should not deal with obscure issues, of no concern to the present audience.

- A speech should deal with the *now*, what is of interest *now*, with perhaps a glimpse into the future.

True, a really skilled speaker can turn the thoughts of an audience towards a new subject of moment. And true, there are 'speeches' intended for entertainment alone, which need to do no more than that.

■ **But any speech made in a business context by a business speaker should produce some sort of change in the interests of the business of the speaker. Even if this is no more than a little dollop of PR.**

Please think about this.

The Political Speech is also very much 'of the moment'. The astute politician—and all politicians need to be astute if they are to stay in office—is always very careful to say what his audience *at the time and place* expects him to say. In this way he can be sure of their support. 'Rah! Rah! Hear, hear!' Support is what he thrives on.

To make an effective speech a politician, especially, has to consider 'audience'. The general opinion has to be appreciated, and the prevailing mood.

Which becomes rather difficult when there is no audience present to talk to, as in TV interviews. And this explains why speeches on TV are generally so dreary and dull. They lack the excitement and the immediacy of a meeting in the local hall, where the speaker gets immediate reaction, so knows at once if he has judged it right or wrong.

And even when it is all in the local hall, but under the hot glare of TV lights, the speaker is aware of the larger unseen audience, so tones it all down. And those in the hall will have been warned to cool it.

To avoid mistaking an audience mood which he has no means of really knowing, a speaker on TV has to stay very bland. And actually say just about nothing, seldom calling for much action either.

You have to Know your Audience. They are important to you.

You want them to know more about *this*?
You want them to change their attitude to *that*?

You want them to change in their course of behaviour on the *other*?

You can do no more than speak to them, suggest, and plead. It is they who will decide whether or not they will change.

There will be more about 'consider your audience' in the next chapter. Your audience is the action part of your effective communication.

> **CHANGE IS BROUGHT ABOUT BY YOUR AUDIENCE.
> NOT BY YOU. YOU CAN DO NO MORE THAN ASK.**

Presentations

A presentation is not another and separate form of communication. Any communication, proposal, sermon, talk, lecture, or speech, can be made into a presentation.

A presentation merely dresses up the message. With flowery language, sound and music, flashing lights, and even dancing girls. All very exciting, but there are real dangers.

Down along Main Street is a store which sells electrical appliances. Into this store comes the representative of a firm which manufactures refrigerators. He shows photos of the new model to the manager of the store, and he hands over a sheet of paper which gives the full technical spec.

The manager glances at the photo. He is not impressed.

'This is exactly the same as last year. All you have done is change the shape of the handle.'

But, of course, this is not the way it is done.

More usually the manager, and lots of other managers, are invited to spend a jolly weekend at some fancy casino. They are wined and dined and on the Saturday evening, after the banquet, the trumpets sound and the curtains part, and there stands 'Miss Refrigerator' dressed in a purple sash.

She introduces 'OUR NEW MODEL' which stands beside

her. (Nobody had noticed it before.) Music! Shouting! Fire-
works! And sore heads the next morning.

When our manager gets back to Main Street and the first
of the new refrigerators arrives, he looks at it and thinks,
'This is the same old crud as last year. All they have done
is change the shape of the handle.'

BEWARE!

If you are *listening* to a presentation, cut through the decorations
to the true message.

If you are *giving* a presentation, make sure that there *is* a message.

■ **A bikini may be pretty.**
■ **But it is the girl inside who counts.**

I have gone to some trouble to describe the various types of spoken
communication. The talk, the lecture, and the speech. My intention
is not to catalogue but to point up the differences. Each is distinct.
Each has its own use.

Which form to use?

You will usually be guided on this.

Suppose that you have been asked to address a group on your
recent trip to Japan.

This is a request for a *talk*. You need only to inform, in an
informal way. So prepare to tell them what you saw, livening it up
a bit by adding a few of your impressions.

An address to the 'International Study Group' on the same
subject? This should be more of a lecture. So make more of
significant facts. Give them something solid to take down in their
notes. Help them to form new opinions and possibly change their
attitude.

A club has invited you as an after-dinner speaker? To speak on
Japan? Fine. The mood of an after-dinner speech is relaxed and

informal—or it should be. After a good dinner people want to be entertained. So entertain them. Tell amusing incidents. Nothing too heavy. All light enough to be forgotten by next day.

■ **In none of these examples should you try to change the beliefs of your listeners, to convert them to Shintoism, for example.**

Nor are you expected to urge that they take the trip to Japan for themselves. (Even if you have been promised a cut by the travel agents.)

PROFIT FROM OPPORTUNITIES TO PRACTISE YOUR SPEAKING

Neither an informal talk/lecture, nor an informal speech, is to be used for the purposes of Conversion or Canvass. This is not expected of you. You are not supposed to be changing anybody on anything and you will not be popular if you try.

This does not mean that the professional or business person wastes time and effort by speaking on informal subjects to informal groups. Far from it. Apart from the fun and social satisfaction, these are ideal opportunities for you to practise your speaking skills.

Far better to practise on a group who are not clients and customers, and who will overlook your errors and mistakes, than to make a mess in front of people who *are* clients and customers, who won't be so tolerant.

Purpose

We are discussing this matter of the 'form of your spoken communication' rather early, before we have even mentioned the mechanics of speaking, and with good reason.

In all communication the first step is to be sure of *purpose*. Which very seldom happens . . .

People stand up and they talk, and they talk quite well, and they would communicate well too if only they had decided exactly what it is they want to say.

You must know your *purpose*. Before you even start to prepare.

Whenever you are called upon to speak, you must first ask yourself:

What is expected of me?
(What have I been asked to do?)

What do I expect of myself?
(What do *I* want to accomplish?)

From your answers to these questions you must determine:

What is it that I expect to change? Is it:

— a Change in Level of Knowledge

— a Change in Attitude

— a Change in Behaviour and Course of Action

You should also consider the particular occasion and the particular audience. The occasion may not be all that momentous—it could be a small meeting called at your place of work. The audience may not be large—it could be one person across a desk. But whenever you consider a communication worth your while to *prepare* then you should ask yourself these questions on your *purpose*. Or you run the risk of waffling on and on to no useful effect.

Once sure of purpose you can decide on form.

> Giving information?—It can be a simple talk.
> Important information?—It should be a lecture.
> To echo 'thoughts of the moment?—A summarising speech.
> Want to get things done?—Then it has to be a solid speech with a definite proposal.

Note that a proposal will always have to give some information too. And be in touch with what is going on. It is a complete form of communication. And the most useful. It informs, it sets attitudes and opinions, then calls for definite change. A proposal moves things along.

Your *Call for Action* starts things moving. (But no calls for impossible actions, please. No 'sermons'.)

So make a clear Proposal whenever you can.

Call for the change which your purpose requires.

As I am doing now.

> I am asking you to take a new view on communication.

> I am asking you to change and improve your techniques to make yourself more effective.

> This is a solid call for action.

> And quite possible.

★ Realization!

At the end of each chapter I will offer a 'Realization!' which I will ask you to change to and accept.

Your Realization for this first chapter is:

> **All this is common-sense and easy.**
> **It can help me.**

SUMMARY:
The Ten Key Points of Chapter 1.

1. *Headline* whatever you have to say.
2. Offer an early *Benefit.*
3. *Speak up* on all occasions.
4. Propose a *Change*!
5. This change must be *Possible.*
6. A *Talk* is 'about something'.
   A *Lecture* is more significant.
   A *Speech* is 'of the moment'. And can produce action.
7. A *Presentation* dresses up but adds nothing.
8. Be sure of your *Purpose.*
9. Decide upon *Form* to suit occasion and audience.
10. Call for *Action* on the change you propose.

Exercise 1

Here are three brief communications. Which is a proposal, which a talk, and which a 'sermon'? (Answers at the end of this chapter.)

1. 'The goose is an amazing bird. It can be a useful sentry as it will cry out loudly if disturbed. In ancient Rome, the sacred geese gave the alarm when the stealthy Gauls tried to scale the walls of the Citadel by night. The dogs heard nothing. There is a lot of talk these days about security. Geese should be used to guard property. They should make more use of geese.'

2. 'We share this earth with the animals. We are all here for a divine purpose. What right has a woman to wear animal fur? Why should innocent animals have to suffer and be killed for her adornment? Whenever you see a woman wearing a fur coat attack her! Beat at her with your fists! Shout your protests!'
3. 'Let's go back to my place. And have some coffee. And relax.'

Exercise 2

I have suggested that you go out and talk to strangers as a useful form of practice, with some element of difficulty to it, as you will be outside of your normal circle.

No doubt many of you won't . . . And the less shy who do, need this practice the least . . .

Here is an alternative. It won't spread sunshine, as does talking to strangers, but it will help you to marshal a message into clear words.

YOU MUST SAY THESE EXERCISES ALOUD!
Suggestions: To a friend. Alone, on a country walk. In your bath, with the water running.

If you can manage to bring a little form into it, all the better.
Example: 'My dog'

'Let me tell you about my dog.
This will make you laugh!'
(Tell dog story)

'Doesn't that make you agree that dogs are almost human?'

But such a definite sequence of Headline, Benefit, Story, and Proposal is not really expected of you at this early stage. Just talk on the subject. For about a minute. That is enough for a start.

Select from these subjects:

My dog.
The car I remember best.
Where you should go on holiday.

Why you should exercise.
The pleasures of my hobby.
My kind of music.
The best meal of the day.
What to do at the week end.
Advice on watching TV.

This may sound to be simple, it may sound to be elementary, but I can assure you that it is not. Especially for the first couple of tries, and especially if you elect to talk 'live' to a friend.

Answers to Exercise 1

Geese.   There is no direct call to the audience to use geese as watch-dogs. 'They should . . .' is the universal vague suggestion. It accomplishes nothing. This is not a proposal. Nor is the information significant enough to rank as a lecture. This is 'about something'. About geese. It is a talk.

Furs.   Laudable sentiments, perhaps. But, even should we agree, this beating and shouting is not a practical suggestion. A 'sermon'.

Cosy Evening.   A genuine proposition. Which is the same as a proposal.

2

Speak up with confidence

Many people find it difficult to speak up, to a group, to strangers, to a group of strangers . . . Especially to a large group of strangers.

It can even, on occasion, be frightening to have to talk to *one* person. To a fierce-looking customer, or to frowning Mr Big from Head Office . . .

To overcome all this you need confidence.
This chapter is about confidence. (The Headline)
It tells you how you can gain confidence. (Your Benefit)

Fear

The absolute horror of knowing that you will have to stand there and say words . . . Or will there *be* words?
Will my mouth open and close like a fish? While no words come out?

Don't think that you are unique if you have this worry. It is universal. When the *Sunday Times* of London conducted a survey on 'My most dreaded fear' the fear of speaking came out on top.

Here are the Top Ten:

Fear of speaking in front of a group	41 %
Fear of heights	32 %
Fear of insects	22 %
Fear of snakes	22 %
Fear of loss of income	22 %
Fear of drowning	22 %
Fear of sickness	19 %
Fear of death	19 %
Fear of flying	18 %
Fear of loneliness	16 %

You will notice that the total percentage is well over 100. This is because most people reported more than one fear.

More interesting is this. All of these fears, except one, are concerned with self-preservation. They are all instinctive. The exception is 'Fear of speaking in front of a group'. This is not instinctive. It is acquired. So how have we acquired it?

I put this mystery to a group at a seminar as a subject for a discussion. And we came to a conclusion.

In their early days at school, little children are made to stand up in class to give their 'news'. Which they gladly do. They lisp out that 'My Daddy says that my Mommy is getting too fat.' They do reveal family secrets like this. They really do. At this young age little children have no problem in speaking up. In fact, teacher's problem is in keeping them quiet. And if they don't have dramatic enough tidings from home to tell they make them up. Which is something else for you to worry about.

Later, they develop a self-awareness. How am I against the others? How do I compare? They also begin to worry. The others are laughing. Are they laughing at me?

At this stage the class divides into two distinct groups. The few extroverts enjoy the laughter, they soak up the applause. They ham it up and become even more out-going.

But the many introverts, they suffer. Their fear of speaking in public has been formed.

Did this ever happen to you? Were you made to speak up while the class laughed?

Maybe the finding of this group was quite wrong. Maybe not . . .

But so many of us have acquired this fear from *somewhere*. Fortunately, however acquired, it is easily lost. Everybody can lose their fear, and can speak up boldly.

I'll prove it.

> Go to the most introverted person you know. Somebody who never speaks up. Who could never say 'boo' to the proverbial goose.
>
> Knock this person down. (Did I mention that they should be smaller than you are?)
>
> When they pick themselves up you will notice that they can express themselves perfectly! The language may not be too good, they may swear a little, but they will say exactly what they want to say. Which is what they think about you.

The reason for this sudden loss of the fear of speaking is of course the sudden stimulation. The sudden excitement. The instant confidence.

■ **You have to be confident if you are to conquer fear!**

Three Essentials for Confidence when Speaking

☆ Excitement, in its more controllable form of *Enthusiasm* is one essential for confidence.

☆ Another essential is mastery of *Technique*. Once you know that you are doing it right you must be content.

☆ And the third essential, which builds up with time and practice, is *Experience*.

You do not need to take my word on this. Prove it for yourself. Think of your favourite game or sport. You are quite happy, quite at ease, quite confident when playing this. Right?

> This is because of your enthusiasm for what you are doing.
> You love it, you enjoy it.
> Also, you know how to play. You have mastered technique.
> And you have done it all before. Successfully. So you have
> the confidence of experience.

In order to build up your enthusiasm in speaking, to chase away those lurking fears, you need to work in these same three areas.

Enthusiasm, Technique, and Experience.

Enthusiasm

> You must be enthusiastic about whatever you say. Enthusi-
> asm is infectious. If you are enthusiastic, then your audience
> will be enthusiastic too.

To which you may reply, 'Fine. I agree. But I am a placid person, always have been. I can be enthusiastic here inside, but my feelings do not show. So how do I *show* this enthusiasm to others?'

Of course you can be enthusiastic. Everybody can, about something. (Family, hobby, achievement, car.) You will be enthusiastic when you talk about these favourite topics *and* it will show, with no effort on your part, no problem at all.

The key to this natural enthusiasm is 'Wanting to share'. The feeling of 'I enjoy this. I must tell others about it so that they will enjoy it too.'

There is also some element of personal pride.

'Let me tell you about what *I* achieved.'

'Let me tell you about *my* new car.'

'New' is another clue. Enthusiasm is strongest when it is about something new.

'Wait until I tell you the wonderful news about our Peter.'

We just have to share our enthusiasm. We just have to tell it to others.

So, where you can, talk about something new that excites you personally. I say 'Where you can' and it all would be so easy if we could choose our own subjects.

But the boss does not say, 'Go and tell them in Accounts what you saw in the Game Reserve.' He says, 'Go and tell them in Accounts how to reconcile the figures', or something mundane like that.

Into which dull subject you will have to bring some enthusiasm.
Or your audience will leave.

They may not leave physically. They may remain sitting there, eyes open. But they will be away in their minds, thinking their own thoughts, and you will have lost them.

Before I give you the well-proven method for making sure that people do sit up and listen to you, excitement in their eyes, enthusiastic, for *any* subject you may have to talk about, let us look at a basic rule of communication:

Do not say what you want to say.
Say what the audience wants to hear.

But, as we have noted, you seldom have your own choice of subject. So what then? Adjust the rule:

■ **SAY WHAT YOU HAVE TO SAY**
■ **IN A WAY THAT YOUR AUDIENCE LIKES TO HEAR**

'Would I really be interested in listening to me?' This is what you must ask yourself. At a very early stage of preparation. While you are working out what you will say.

Common-sense again!

What do people really like to hear? What do you? Let's make a list.

— I want to hear about things that affect me.
— I want it to be told in a lively fashion.
— It must always be *interesting*.

There is a simple way to attain this. There is a principle which will enable you to make any subject affect your audience, and be lively, and be interesting. People like to hear about people. So:—

TALK ABOUT PEOPLE NOT THINGS

If your subject is a 'thing' you can still do it.

Connect people to the thing.
'This is about the new office intercom and how it will affect you.'

Put people into the thing.
'Let me tell you what the new model will be like to drive.'

Put things into people.
'We are bringing out new flavours, which everybody will want to try.'

Not only do people like to hear about people, they like especially to hear about themselves.

'This is what I want to talk about, and how it affects *you*.'

Two further useful hints:

Tell anecdotes

Some story (not too long) about 'My first encounter with unreconciled accounts, and how it affected me.'

Anecdotes are always so useful. They are normally light and often humorous. They are easy to remember and they are easy to tell. More important, anecdotes are about people. And they get you excited. This immediately shows in your voice and in the way your hands move. You share your *enthusiasm*. (You can't tell a story without moving your hands, now can you?)

Some years ago I was being driven by a Frenchman, near Paris, in a very fast car. I leaned sideways to look at the instruments.

'What is the speed limit on this highway?' I asked.

'One hundred and forty kilometers . . .'

'But you are doing one hundred and eighty.'

He lifted both hands from the wheel, momentarily, to make a Gallic gesture.

'In France,' he shrugged, 'the rules are made to be bro-ken.'

This is a good anecdote for several reasons:

- It fits in.

- It raises a smile.

- It is short.

- It makes a point.

And the point it makes is this. The last thing I want to do is turn out hordes of walking-talking standard communicators. Each one of you must remain an individual. So take note of the Rules, which I set down throughout this book, but feel free to break them when you feel the need to arise. **AND** . . . Break the rules *only when you are sure of what you are doing.*

After you have told a perfectly marvellous anecdote which has gone down very well, it is a great temptation to try to repeat the success. To tell another immediately. Don't. The currants should be spread in the bun. Too many, too close together, can lead to indigestion.

No anecdote need be entirely true. All anecdotes can be improved upon. Many are quite easily converted to suit your present needs.

It may have been your brother who had the experience with the elephant. But if the story can be made to fit, you use it. Say, 'This happened to me.'

Smile! As you talk.

I am not a natural smiler. I wish I were. I wish I had an unforced and *natural* smile. It is a real asset. Nothing relaxes your audience faster than your smile. A smile is infectious. So they will smile back (or at least some of them will) and that will help you. Smiles are as infectious as enthusiasm.

At this point in the course, last year, any smile was taken off my face. A sudden question brought me up short. 'What,' I was asked, 'do you do when you have to tell bad news?' 'You are thinking well,' I said. 'You are appreciating a problem.'

For you cannot very well smile when telling people that their bonus is to be cut this year. Nor will they be very interested in your sympathy. Even though you do tell them an hilarious story about one Christmas when you yourself were broke . . .

So how *do* you tell bad news in a way that people will like to hear?

People do not turn away from hearing bad news *when it affects them.* They may not be wildly enthusiastic, but they will listen attentively. They want to know by how much their bonus has been cut, and the reasons why. They want it straight.

So do not be scared to give bad news. Do not display the often-seen apologetic air and complete lack of confidence.

There is no point in telling bad news to people when it does not affect them. Yet this too often happens. Audiences have little enthusiasm for prophets of general doom. And serve such prophets right.

Understandably, it is also difficult to be enthusiastic when giving out boring information. Such as explaining the new procedure for reconciling the accounts.

So say at the start, 'This affects you. Head Office says that this is the way it is to be done.'

As with bad news, they may not be wildly enthusiastic. But they will realise that it is to their benefit to listen and be interested.

To keep them interested, keep talking about people (them), tell amusing anecdotes (as relevant as possible) and do remember to smile!

Your efforts could even arouse a little audience enthusiasm. Which would be great for your confidence. You were given a difficult assignment, and you have found a way to make it work.

Of course, if the members of an audience are not involved in the subject which you have to talk about, then there is no way that you can arouse their enthusiasm, or even their interest. It is no good offering the wrong message to the wrong audience. Yet this happens surprisingly often.

Salespeople need to show enthusiasm when they talk about their wares. Which is made easier when there is a new product to offer. And made difficult when there has been nothing new for ages.

The same story to tell . . . Over and over and over . . . It becomes so boring to you and it shows. The customers may even yawn.

The same can happen with any verbal communication that has to be repeated. ('You did so well with your explanation of the new way to reconcile the accounts. So now I want you to go round all the branches and do the same.')

If you can retain your enthusiasm on an umpteenth repeat then you are an ace. Your future is sure. But you can be bored if you wish. It does not matter. *Provided that you do not appear to be bored.* Audiences are wizards at detecting any sign of your boredom. They notice it immediately.

An actor is faced with the same problem. An actor has to appear fresh while delivering the same lines night after night. How do they manage this? I asked an actor and was told:

'The audience changes. And each audience is unique. So I pick up their reactions, I watch, I listen. Then I modify my

delivery and I alter my bits of business. I try to feed my
material to this new audience in a way that I feel they enjoy.
It is quite a challenge, but it can be done, and it works. I am
working just for them and they seem to know. They respond.'

You can do the same. Modify your message, and the way you tell
it, to suit each new audience. Watch their reactions. Tell them in
the way they want it told.

And you do have two advantages over the actor. You are not
stuck with the exact same lines each time, as he is. And you do
know something about each audience in advance, so you can plan.
What is this next group likely to be like? How will this next
customer be different? Plan. Prepare. What is the best way to hold
the interest the next time I give this same spiel?

Making your message apply specifically to each particular audience is not easy. It is hard work. But 'meeting audience need' is a
mark of your competence and a key to your confidence. And a route
to sure success.

There will be more on meeting the needs of your audience in the
next chapter.

Technique

We have spent some time on ways to build up your confidence by
being sure of your enthusiasm. It is important. The second require-
ment for confidence, if you remember that far back, is to be sure
of your technique.

A later chapter, 'Use More than Words', will deal fully on how
you should speak. At this earlier stage I would like to offer some
very useful short tips which will instantly boost your confidence.

Know your first sentence off by heart.

This is a great help. You know that you will not go 'er . . . er . . .'
and then dry up. You will have something definite to say, and while

you are saying it the butterflies will settle, you will work out what it is you want to say next, and you will be off. Not only that. You will know that you have a strong opening. So why not learn your last sentence as well? Then you will be sure of a strong ending, too.

Use the four P's.

Pitch, Pace, and Pause. And Projection.

Pitch: We have all heard those speakers who go on-and-on-in-a-monotone with a voice that is dreary and dull. Boring . . .
There is an easy way to avoid this, which has already been hinted at. Be *excited* about all that you have to tell. 'This is *special.* Listen to *this.*'
(Say that quick message out loud. You can't say it in a flat voice, now can you?)
No need to worry about whether your voice is going 'up and down'. Put life into your subject and life will come into your voice. Automatically.

To check on your own 'pitch performance' listen to a playback of yourself on a tape recorder. Do you sound alive? Or dreary? Be honest now.
You know the cure if needed. Show *excitement!* (Practice telling exciting stories to a tape recorder. But don't over-do it. Don't force.) Also listen for a drop in pitch at the end of each sentence. This is a common fault with many speakers, and something else which you may need to work on.

Pace: Most inexperienced speakers speak far too fast. This is often due to nervousness. There is a strong urge to 'get it over with'.
There is also a pace/age relationship. Young people tend to talk fast. Their mental agility is at its peak, they can think quickly and they can speak quickly, so they do. Do you speak too fast? Ask your friends. Listen to yourself on a tape recorder. If you do tend

to go off at a fast pace, then try to speak more deliberately. **S-L-O-W** down.

Pause: In the written word, punctuation is essential. A solid page of words, no breaks at all, would be very difficult to understand. So the page is separated into paragraphs, there are stops between sentences, and commas too.

For easy understanding of the spoken words, some form of punctuation is just as important. This punctuation takes the form of pauses.

When speaking, you should make a definite and quite lengthy pause between your 'paragraphs' each of which should contain a separate message. These pauses give the members of your audience the chance to organise their thoughts and also—which is often overlooked—pauses give *you* the opportunity to organise too. To think out what next you want to say.

You can stop speaking for quite a long time. A pause of seven or eight seconds may seem like an eternity, to you standing there. You may even fear that they will think that you have dried up.

But such pauses are quite acceptable, and seem quite normal, to any audience.

• Pause for a long measure between your 'pieces of message'.

• Pause for a shorter time between each sentence.

• Pause, very briefly, for 'comma' breaks.

You may also, if you wish, pause occasionally between each word. Which — adds — emphasis.

Projection: 'Project your voice to the back of the audience'. This is very easy to say as to 'what'. But not so easy to explain as to 'how'. A voice-training teacher will show you how. So will a singing coach. On your own, try these hints and practise, and you should gain the knack:

—Speak as loud as you can without shouting.

—Open your lips and bounce your voice off the roof of your mouth.

—'Think' your voice to the back of the hall.

Never ever ask, 'Can you hear me at the back?' This is the mark of the amateur. The experienced speaker *knows* how far the voice is carrying.

If you are offered a mike in a large hall, use it, but remember that use of a microphone will always slow you down. Which may not be such a bad thing . . .

Experience

Nothing builds confidence like experience. The first time you have to confront an angry customer, the first time you have to speak at a meeting, the first time you stand to speak to a crowd, is definitely the worst. From then on it will go easier.

PROFIT FROM YOUR INCREASED CONFIDENCE

The simple message is this:

☆ Take advantage of every opportunity to speak.

☆ Practise and use the techniques given in this book as often as you can.

The area where you are likely to need most practice, and from which you will gain most benefit when you have it right, is the thoughts/words interface. Some explanation . . .

The Perilous Path

The route for thoughts going from your mind into the minds of others is quite perilous. There are two awesome barriers.

• The first is where your thoughts are turned into words, which we will discuss now.

• This second is where words are turned back into thoughts, which we will discuss under listening.

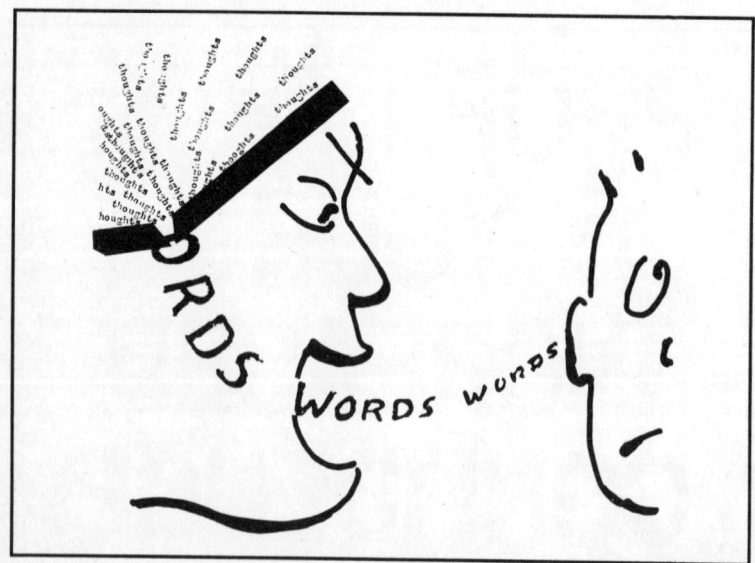

The Perilous Path

'Thoughts are like tapestry in the bale, with figures rolled all together.
But speech is like tapestry unfolded, where the figures stand out all distinct.'

Thermistocles. (So perceptive! So long ago.)

Our ideas do not start off as words. They start off, in our minds, as thoughts. These thoughts come crowding, very fast indeed.

In order to transmit our thoughts to other people we have to transform them into words, to be spoken out. And into only a limited quantity of words, at that.

For we think fast, many thoughts. We speak slowly, few words.

The transformation point I have described as a barrier. It is better described as a funnel. It has to funnel all those teeming thoughts, to emerge as a few well-chosen words.

And, apart from the speed-change problem, there is also the sheer *difficulty* of turning the one into the other.

This process comes naturally to us, to a certain extent.

It can be improved upon. As with many other natural processes, like running, or dexterity, or anything else that can be learned, it may be vastly improved by being properly trained.

'I know exactly what I want to say, but I don't seem to be able to put my thoughts into words.'

How often have you heard this? Or said it yourself? Successful thoughts-to-words comes from practice. And more practice ... To speed the process I have devised a series of exercises, which are coming up now. But, just before we come to these:

 *Realization!*

**Any fear I may have of speaking in public is not unique.
I can cure it with confidence.**

SUMMARY: The Ten Key Points of Chapter 2.

1. Fear of speaking is universal.
2. *Everybody* can speak up if excited.
3. *Confidence* conquers fear.
4. Confidence comes from *Enthusiasm.*
5. Confidence comes from mastery of *Technique.*
6. Confidence comes from *Experience.*
7. Be *interesting* for your audience.
8. Talk about *People* not things.
9. *Project* your voice. Vary *Pitch*, use *Pace* and *Pauses.*
10. Practise turning *Thoughts* into *Words.*

EXERCISES

1. Walk with a companion along a street or a stretch of road which you know well. Describe aloud the things you pass. These will be familiar objects, easy to talk about. The purpose is to use the 'observation' part of the brain while turning your thoughts into words. Now let your companion have a turn.
2. Same again, but now you both sit indoors in comfort. Describe to each other what you saw on that walk. You are now using the 'memory' part of the brain.
3. More difficult, but potentially the most useful. Describe that same scene, as you imagine it to have been fifty years ago. You are now exercising 'imagination'.

3

Prepare with care

This chapter will show you:

- How to organise what you want to say.

- How to edit your material.

- How to speak without notes.

With these skills you will be able to put across your message in a competent and confident manner.

You will recognise the above as the familiar 'Headline' and 'Benefit'.

We now proceed to a third element which is most useful whenever you begin to speak.

The 'Relaxer'.

> 'Words slip out so easily for me . . .
>
> I use plenty of oil on my salad.'

This relaxer can be a quick quip or a short joke. It works like this. All audiences are concerned and a little apprehensive when first you stand to speak. They are concerned for you. They really are. They worry that you might make a mess of things. They sit tense.

So use a light remark to make them smile. And then they can relax.

More important, now that they are relaxed *you can relax too*. For you are a little tensed up whenever you start to speak, aren't you? Everybody is. This is quite normal. If you are not a little nervous and tense, then your audience is in for a slack performance.

It is not necessary to tell a long and involved Van der Merwe story. In fact nothing long and involved at all. All you need is something short and simple, and relevant if possible, that will raise a smile.

I heard a good example recently. A speaker had been introduced as 'Speaking with an inner fire.' He followed up on this with, 'Ah, so that's what it is. And I always thought it was heartburn.'

This sounded to be ad-libbed and it probably was. But no need to worry if you can't snap back as wittily. Prepare some suitable 'ad-libs'.

> 'I'll take a sip of water to stop my words from being dry.'
> 'Let me give you a warm welcome on this cold morning.'
> 'I've always wanted to meet you. You sound so friendly on the phone.'

Your relaxer can be as simple as these. It does not have to be a joke.

You must smile yourself when you say it! We have taken note of the value of your smile before. While giving your relaxer your smile is essential.

They may not be sure whether they should smile themselves or not. So cue them. Smile.

The full set of components for your effective opening is:

- Headline (You tell them what it is about)

- Benefit (You tell them what's in it for them)

- Relaxer (You put them at their ease)

This sequence may be varied and will still work well. Your opening will start you off effectively. Provided that all three elements are used.

There is a school of thought that does not agree with this method . . .

They feel it is essential to **STARTLE THE AUDIENCE OUT OF THEIR DOZINESS**. First off. As they stand to speak.

So they **WAKE THE AUDIENCE UP**. They slap the table, they scream 'I have a message for you!' and one man, at a speaking contest I was judging in East London, fired a blank cartridge into the floor.

This woke me up all right. I jumped right out of my seat. I do not remember what this particular speaker spoke about but I do remember his shock opening, after all these years.

In my experience you do not need to wake your audiences up. They are normally awake and quite alert when first you start to speak. Although you may have problems later . . .

Another school of thought feels that you should start off with a question. Their theory is that asking a question raises interest.

'Do you know the most common classification of butterfly in South Africa?'

The problem with such a quiz opening is that in order to work the question has to be difficult. It has to show the speaker as being superior, as knowing much more than the audience, and this can annoy people.

There is also the real risk with a specialised, tricky, or obtuse question, that nobody may care what the answer is, anyway.

Yet another group maintains, 'Always start at the beginning,' and this, at a first glance, would seem to be rather sensible and logical.

But let's see how this worked out at a First Aid lesson which I attended recently.

'First make sure that the air passages are clear and free of mucus.'
Ugh! Puts us off right away.

So rather:
'I am going to show you the proper way to restore breathing.
It is important that you know this. You may need such
knowledge in an unexpected emergency. It could help you
to save a human life.'
Now we know what it is about. Now we can understand what
we can gain. Now we are motivated to listen, even to the
unpleasant parts.

Notice that no 'Relaxer' is suggested here. It would break the mood
of a serious introduction. No jokes at a funeral. And no fixed rules
in Effective Communication.

You can break the 'Opening' rules of Headline/Benefit/Relaxer
at an informal meeting or in conversation. In fact you have to. You
have to grab and hold interest. Or be ignored.

'Did I tell you about the time I was swimming at a beach on
the South Coast when I was on holiday. It was quite late in
the evening and most of the people had gone and . . .'

Useless. The speaker might as well stop there. Nobody is listening.
They have gone, too. Rather:

'I was once bumped by a shark.'

Start with the punch-line. Then, as they turn to you, open-mouthed
and attentive, fill in the rest. This same technique—start with the
significant, as a newspaper story does—can be useful on more
formal speaking occasions, too. When a speaker comes to me after
the event to ask, 'How did I go?' I often produce a question of my
own:

'At what point did you feel that you grabbed your audience?'

'Oh, that's easy. When I told them that productivity can be
increased by 30 %. I knew I had their interest there.'

'So might it not have been better to *start* with the exciting
figure? And then work back?'

The flash-back technique. Start with an arresting event then fill in what happened before. Used in films. Used in short stories. Very successfully.

Useful particularly whenever you have a narrative to recount. Grab their interest first, then tell the rest.

No fixed rules, all common-sense. Break the rules by all means, once you are sure of what you are doing.

But mostly, whenever you are called upon to 'say a few words' I strongly suggest that you start off with the old tried and reliable. Headline, Benefit, and Relaxer.

It always works.

Finally, one more look at the importance of 'Headline'. (And never say 'Finally . . .' more than three times!)

You know your subject, you have researched it, you have prepared thoroughly, you have gone through your words over and over in your mind, you have rehearsed aloud, in front of a mirror, to the cat . . .

So you know what it is that you are going to talk about, and possibly the cat knows. But your poor audience, they have not a clue. Until you tell them.

So do remember to Headline.

How do I come across?

Analysis after the event is always educational. I used to wonder why it was that whenever I spoke, the effect upon the audience was always somewhat less than I had expected.

So I asked people. 'How do I come across?'

Most mumbled reassuring pleasantries. Which helped me not at all.

Then one man said: 'You try to cover too much ground and you speak in a muddle.'

Too much material . . . and muddled . . . the same faults which I notice so often in others . . . But which I have now corrected in myself. (How do I know this? That I have improved? Again, I ask people.)

In order to make sure that I always use the most significant material, edited into a tight and logical sequence, I devised a new method for preparation.

Over the years I have developed and refined this 'Ten Point Plan' to make it even easier to use, and to make it more efficient. I have taught this plan to very many people. All report that they apply it with success.

So here, for the very first time in print, is the **TEN-POINT PLAN**. Ready to spread its usefulness even wider.

But first, two important considerations:

1. Know your Purpose

We have already mentioned purpose. I make no apology for emphasising purpose again. You have to be sure of what it is that you want to accomplish before you can even start to think about what you are going to say.

- What is expected of me?

- What do I expect of myself?

- What do I seek to change?

2. Consider your Audience

■ **Say what you have to say.**
■ **In a way that the audience wants to hear.**

Different audiences will appreciate different benefits in whatever it is that you have to tell them. So you may have to alter, or change emphasis, or revise entirely, the benefits that you intend to offer.

The smaller the group you talk to, the closer on target you can be. With a message going to a one-person audience being the most flexible, and potentially the strongest of all.

Here's a very short example. The audience is a protective secretary.

> 'Is the boss in?'
> 'What do you want with him?'
> 'I want to sell him on something.'
> 'He's extremely busy.'
> '. . . something that could make him a lot of money.'
> 'He might be able to spare a moment.'
> 'This interview could earn you his thanks for life.'
> 'Go straight through.'

The right form of the benefit, right for each particular audience, can work wonders.

IMPORTANT PRINCIPLE:

- **Different audiences appreciate different benefits.**
- **To suit a particular audience, you may need to offer an alternative 'What's in it for you' on the same subject.**

Not only the benefit may have to vary with the audience, you may need to vary the emphasis of your main message too.

Think of yourself in this situation:

Your purpose 'To tell people about my job'.

Your various audiences being:

1. A group of schoolchildren.
2. Colleagues in the same line of business.
3. A chance acquaintance, met on holiday.

Same job. Your job doesn't change. *But the way you talk about it to these various people will.*

IMPORTANT PRINCIPLE:

> **You may have to vary the *emphasis of your message* to suit the particular interests of your audience.**

Example:

Consider the plight of the site foreman on the Tower of Pisa job. To the Duke he reports:

'It is true that the tower is tilting slightly. But the work will be completed on time. There will be no extra cost.'

To the representative of the Stone-chippers Union:

'It is true that the tower is tilting slightly. But there is no risk to the workmen. Danger money will not be paid. Work will continue as usual.

To the local odd-ball:

'I do appreciate your point. It is not the tower that is crooked, but the *town.* Thank you for bringing this to my attention.'

I have had some fun composing a modern-style press release for this ancient incident:

Dateline Pisa.
'The prestigious new tower will be opened by the Duke of Bologna on Tuesday. Speaking from his attractive palace and surrounded by his attractive family, the Duke said that he did not think that taxes would have to be increased again this year. The tower is leaning slightly.'

Such exercises are not only fun. They are very good training for the imagination.

IMPORTANT PRINCIPLE:

> **Your examples gain by being imaginative.**
> **They are easier to visualise. And so easier to understand.**

Another example, in selling and closer to home. This illustrates how both benefit, and direction of message, can be adjusted.

- You sell a special type of beam, used in roofing. To the rich man, wanting a wide garage to house his new sports car, his caravan, and his speedboat, you stress 'Economy'. He is rich but he is penny-pinching. That's how he got to be rich.

- To the dear old lady, wanting to build a mausoleum for poor little Fido, her lately deceased miniature poodle who had the misfortune to be trodden on, you stress 'Long lasting'. She never wants anything to fall on poor little Fido ever again.

So . . .

Purpose stays the same—But the benefit you offer can alter.

Message stays broadly the same—But the emphasis may alter.

Depending upon your 'audience'.

And . . .

■ **It is vital to 'Know your Purpose'.**
It is vital to 'Consider your Audience'.

⇨ Earlier on I gained your attention by telling you of something good coming up. Something to your own benefit. The Ten-Point Plan. I then back-tracked to emphasise some essentials which you need to understand before you can make best use of the plan. This is 'State the most interesting point first, then back-track'. One of our techniques in action . . .

We now move forward.

PROFIT FROM PLANNING YOUR MESSAGE

Ten-Point Plan for Preparing a Proposal

Your proposal can be to a group large or small, in business or socially, to a committee, in debate . . .

The essential is that there is a change which you want to bring about, by standing up and talking. And you have had some advance notice, so there is the opportunity to prepare.

The Ten Points are divided into three groups:
Three of Opening, which you already know:
1. State Headline
2. Give Benefit
3. Use Relaxer

Followed by five points of Body:
4.
5.

6.

7.

8.

With finally, two points of Closure:

9. Summarise.

10. Appeal for Change.

For an example subject we are going to speak on 'Why you should not smoke'. A straightforward topic. A clear-cut purpose.

For an example audience we are going to speak to a group of youngsters, the members of the youth section of a tennis club. A straightforward assembly. A clearly-defined group.

'Say what you want to say'

We want to warn them of the serious consequences of the smoking of tobacco.

'In a way that the audience wants to hear'

What interests them? Themselves, their youth, their health. They are likely to be eager for advice on their personal problems, such as to smoke or not to smoke. Provided they are not *told* what they should do.

Which is a short and accurate enough analysis of the *general trend* likely in this particular audience.

HEADLINE:

'We are going to discuss the effects of the smoking of tobacco.'

Key-Phrase: **DISCUSS TOBACCO**

It is always better to use 'we', 'us', and 'our' rather than 'I', 'me', and 'my'. There is more a sense of sharing in the subject, less 'Let me tell you . . .'

In the same way 'going to discuss'. I will not be dictating to you, I will not offer a solution, cut and dried. We will reach our decision together.

BENEFIT:

'We are going to talk about you. About your most precious possessions. Your young bodies and your good health.'

Key-Phrase: **PRECIOUS POSSESSIONS**

'What's in it for them'. This is going to be about their health and about their bodies.

Two subjects of great interest to them all.

RELAXER:

Small problem here. This is a serious subject so we have set off in serious mood. If we were now to introduce a light aside it would destroy that mood. No jokes at a funeral, remember.

The basic purpose of the 'Relaxer' is to establish rapport, and there are other ways of doing this. One of the best is the tried-and-tested invitation for audience participation.

So ask a question, to be answered by a show of hands.

'How many of you have tried smoking already?'

Key-phrase: **AUDIENCE SMOKE?**

Which is not so clever, now that I think it over . . . Many of those who do smoke will not admit to this. And some of those who don't may indicate that they do, out of bravado. While the majority will decide: 'I don't smoke. This doesn't concern me.' And they will turn off mentally and leave you.

Better to ask: 'How many of you have a good friend who smokes?'

This should raise a good show of hands. And it will raise their interest.

'Now listen carefully. I am going to give some very good reasons why they should stop. You will be able to help them by passing the message on.'

Rapport. We are going to do a good deed together. And the 'friend who smokes' of that blue-eyed thirteen-year-old in the front row might well be herself!

Some explanation of the Key-Phrases:

As well as *organising* your material, this plan also *prompts* you for your telling of it.

Write the three Key-Phrases for this opening on a piece of card. Boldly, with bright felt-pen, in big letters. Our example phrases being:

DISCUSS TOBACCO
PRECIOUS POSSESSIONS
AUDIENCE SMOKE?

From a glance at this card you will be cued to deliver the three points of this particular opening.

Headline . . . Benefit . . . Relaxer . . .

Easy, isn't it?

This is all you need for your opening. Three points. But . . .

BEWARE!

It is a great temptation to overdo your start-up, to make too much of the introduction.

Many speakers make this mistake. They think up a number of good openings—and then they use the lot. With the result that the message proper doesn't start to come through for some time, after the audience has become restless.

You may well be able to think up several openings, all good. But all except one is superfluous.

The **BODY** of the piece.

Apart from their over-long openings, and as we have already noted, very many speakers use far too much material. There is so much that they want to tell, so many points to be covered. They talk on and on and on . . . repetitious . . . irrelevancies . . . no logical order . . . too much material . . . too little editing . . .

Avoid this trap.

☆ *Consider* all the material you can find.

☆ *Use* only the selection that works.

So let us set out a whole series of points concerning 'Why you should not smoke' and gathered from all over.

— Responsible bodies attempt to curb smoking. They have evidence of the harm it can cause.

— Smoking causes lung cancer. This leads to much suffering.

— The story of Sir Walter Raleigh. His servant had never seen anybody smoking a pipe before so he threw a bucket of water over his master.

— Fewer people smoke today. Fear of damage to the health is a prime reason for this decline.

— Land and facilities used for the growing of tobacco could be better used for growing food.

— 'It won't happen to me.' Smokers have a fatalistic outlook.

— Smokers never look all that happy. Can there be real pleasure in tobacco?

— Tobacco contains a dangerous drug. If it were to be discovered as new today it would be banned outright.

— Tobacco affects the nervous system. It slows down reaction
time.
— Smoking causes fires. We would all pay less insurance against
fire if there were no smokers.

So there are ten points on the subject, very mixed and all in briefest
outline. Many more could no doubt be added, but ten are sufficient
to illustrate the selection process.

We have to bring that total down to no more than five.

IMPORTANT RULE:
Three to *Five* points about one subject are quite enough.
Never try to use *more than five.*
Or you sow confusion . . .

Considerations for selection:
— The first point should be especially strong.
— Early points should change level of knowledge.
— There should be a definite and logical sequence.
— Later points should change attitude.
— The last point should be reasonably strong. (You do not want
to fade away . . .)

Not forgetting
— The suitability of each point to the advancement of your pur-
pose.
— The interests of this particular audience.

I prefer to start off with a **BLOCKBUSTER**. Bold enough and
startling enough to make them all sit up.

The 'BLOCKBUSTER':
You are standing on a bridge over a stream.
You wish to attract the attention of the little fish, swimming
so carefree below.
You drop a small pebble. The fish flurry for a moment, then

settle back to normal.
Another pebble . . . same effect.
So you go to fetch a large boulder. You stagger back with it, rest it for a moment on the parapet, then you drop it S-P-L-A-S-H!!! to the water below. *Now* they notice. Now you have their attention.

A good strong point from our list is the one about economic waste, about all the land and facilities used for growing tobacco that could be put to better use for the production of food.

This could be a blockbuster to some audiences. A bunch of economists, perhaps. But for our youthful tennis club members I think I would prefer to use the horrors of lung cancer. A case history, of someone I knew, who died young.

My own selection—after the 1, 2, 3 introduction—would be:
4. Dangers of lung cancer
5. Use of tobacco slows your performance.
6. Waste of resources to produce a 'weed'.
7. Danger of fire. (This would have higher priority to an older audience, who pay high insurance premiums.)

All of the above change 'level of knowledge' and lead up to a call for 'change of attitude':
8. Responsible bodies, after much investigation, report that use of tobacco causes harm. You can only agree with them.

The Key-phrases for your prompt card being:

LUNG CANCER
SLOW PERFORMANCE
ECONOMIC WASTE
FIRE DANGER
SMOKING HARMS

Should you find yourself unable to summarise a point as a short Key-phrase, then look closely at that point. It is likely to be too involved, or too complicated, or otherwise unclear.

A good clear point can always be summarised in one or two clear words.

It can also be expanded and enlarged upon, illustrated with examples, proved with proofs . . .

But it must never deviate from the purpose in hand.

Nor should a point be allowed to merge with another and blur.

MAKE AND COMPLETE EACH SEPARATE POINT THEN MOVE ON TO THE NEXT

This is where so many speakers fall down. They 'scatter-shot' with bits and pieces taken from all over. They should rather start off with one powerful blockbuster, then follow up on this advantage with a cannonade of strong and complete arguments.

An easy method for physically sorting your points into best order is to write each on a separate card. Or you could make use of a computer database, but this would seem to be an over-involved complication.

THE SUMMARY:

Sam Goldwyn, the film producer, was credited with some amazing pronouncements, most of which he probably did not make.

'Include me out.'
'My wife has such beautiful hands. I'm thinking of having a bust made of them.'
'Have him say some fresh clichés.'

But what he *did* say, and which was clear and unmuddled, was about film-making.

'When making a movie, first tell 'em what you are going to do, then do it, then tell 'em what you have done.'

Which gives the audience three chances to gather in the message . . .

We can do the same when we speak.

> Tell them what you are going to talk about.
> Tell it.
> Tell them what you said.

Which last is the **SUMMARY**:

9. 'I have shown you the harm caused by this evil weed.'

   Key-Phrase: **HARM CAUSED**

This will, of course, be expanded into more than one sentence. It has to have a little detail. But it must not be puffed out to be too long . . .

APPEAL:

As this is a proposition, a proposal, proposing a change in behaviour ('Do not smoke tobacco') you must close off with an *appeal for this change.*

You have to appeal. You have to ask. People are lazy. They do not make changes on their own.

It is effective if the appeal can take the form of an 'arm twister'. Which is an 'offer that they cannot refuse'.

The 'arm twister':

> Little girl writes to a chocolate factory.

> Dear Mr Chocolate Man,
> Please would you make me a piece of pink chocolate. I would very much like this piece of pink chocolate. Please send my piece of pink chocolate to my house. The address of my house for you to send my piece of pink chocolate to, is . . .

> No ways will she get her pink chocolate. The best she can expect is a nice letter from Sales Promotion and a small slab of boring old brown chocolate.

> But wait. She has added a post script . . .
> My Daddy says that he plays golf with you. My Daddy says that he has lots of shares in your Company.

Now she will get her pink chocolate!

The essential for any good arm twister is that it must be an attractive offer of barter. 'It will cost you little to gain much.'

You cannot always think of good arm twisters, of course. But when you can by all means use them.

Our arm twister appeal, the offer which the youngsters at our tennis club should find hard to refuse, because it offers them so much for so little, is:

10. 'Why sabotage your own precious health? Do not smoke.'
Key-Phrase: **LOOK AFTER HEALTH**

You are now fully prepared.

From your cue-card with its complete list of Key-Phrases you will be prompted to give your ten points, all in the correct order, nothing left out.

'I forgot the best part!'
There is nothing so devastating as sitting down, suddenly to realise this. Your cue-card will really help. You can avoid such embarrassment.

The ten Key-Phrases for our example are:

DISCUSS TOBACCO
PRECIOUS POSSESSION
FRIENDS SMOKE?

LUNG CANCER
SLOW PERFORMANCE
ECONOMIC WASTE
FIRE DANGER
SMOKING HARMS

HARM CAUSED
LOOK AFTER HEALTH

It is a simple further step to reduce these Key-phrases to single Key-*words*, which can serve to prompt you just as well.

TOBACCO
POSSESSION
FRIENDS

CANCER
PERFORMANCE
WASTE
FIRE
CURBED

HARM
HEALTH

You can *memorise* a short list of words like this, can't you. And throw away your card.

You can now deliver quite a long spoken message, all in sequence, nothing left out, from *memory*.

No need to look down to read. No need to take glasses off, put them on, take them off. No barrier between you and your audience.

This does make a very big difference, believe me. Both to you and to them.

☆ You find yourself keeping in closer touch.

☆ They see you as a professional speaker.

So 'speak free'. Although you might like the re-assurance of knowing that you have kept your cue-card in your pocket, just in case!

Note: A blank form of work-sheet for the Ten-point Plan has been set out in these pages. You might like to make some larger copies for your own use. This is to help you to plan and prepare, to produce your own cue-sheets.

10-POINT PLAN
FOR PREPARING YOUR SPOKEN COMMUNICATION

Opening	Keys
1. **HEADLINE**	
2. **BENEFIT**	
3. **RELAXER**	

Body	
4.	
5.	
6.	
7.	
8.	

Close	
9. **SUMMARY**	
10. **APPEAL**	

Modules

It may well happen that your material is too long and too complex to be satisfactorily edited down into only ten points. In which case I suggest the use of modules. Break into several sections, each to use the standard ten-point format.

A two-module assembly would go together like this:

> Overall Headline
> Overall Benefit
> Relaxer
>   Headline for module 1
>   Benefit for module 1
>   3–5 main points
>   Summary of module 1
>   Appeal for module 1
>   Headline for module 2
>   Benefit for module 2
>   3–5 main points
>   Summary for module 2
>   Appeal for module 2
> Overall Summary
> Overall Appeal

I would not recommend that you go to more than three modules, certainly not in a single session. If you really do have that much material, and you do have to tell it all, you should give your audience some break, to stretch and breathe deep and have tea, before you start up again.

Length

I am often asked, 'This is my subject, this is my purpose, this is my audience. How long should I talk?' The slick quick answer is, 'For as long as it takes.' A more intelligent reply would be, 'For as long as the audience can take it.'

You can talk on and on for ever . . . But how long you can continue to speak *effectively* does depend upon how long your audience stays with you.

Once you note the classic signs of boredom—and you should be watching closely—the movements, the looking around, the half-stifled yawns, you have to do something.

You have three choices:

1. Close off quickly and sit down.
2. Drop the present point. Switch to the next.
3. Repeat, so that they will understand better.

This third choice is the one most often selected.

N.B. It does not work.

Of course, the length of your discourse is very often determined for you. You receive the programme for the seminar and you find that they have spelt your name incorrectly and that you have been allocated half an hour to speak about something indefinite like 'Accounts'.

This is all wrong. Those who arrange seminars should approach each speaker, discuss subject and scope, and then ask, 'How much time will you need?'

SUMMARY: The Ten Key Points of Chapter 3.

1. *Relax* your audience with a quick smile.
2. Whenever you have to speak, *Know your Purpose.*
3. Whenever you have to speak, *Consider your Audience.*
4. To suit your message to each audience vary the *Emphasis.*
5. *Imaginative* examples are easy to visualise.
6. The Ten-Point Plan:
   Three points of opening.
   Three to Five points of body.
   Two points of closing.
7. Use *Blockbusters* and *Arm twisters.*

8. Break long discourses into *Modules*.

9. *Summarise*.

10. You have to *Appeal* for the change you desire.

Appeal

To make your message more effective please try the Ten-point Plan for your preparation.

You have much to gain for little effort.

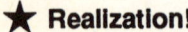 **Realization!**

> **All this makes good sense.**
> **I will try it.**

EXERCISE

You can start now. Prepare some material of your own choice, your own subject, your own message, your own purpose, using the Ten-point Plan.

To gain least benefit, prepare but never use . . .

To gain most benefit, find an audience. Speak to them, for real.

— Perhaps there is a group you should be addressing anyway, in connection with your work?

— Or could you volunteer to say a few words at a meeting of some club or society?

— Maybe a group of friends will listen to you?

— Even family?

Find *some* live audience.

Consider this audience. (Needs, outlook, interests.)

Adjust your message to suit.

Prepare well. (Gather material, edit, organise.)

List your Key-Phrases. Memorise first and last sentences.

Stand up. Relax them with, 'Let me first take a sip of water so I won't give you a dry talk.' Or something like that.
And off you go!
Good Luck.

4

Learn to listen

To upset somebody, we have only to say:

'You have no sense of humour.'

Almost as effective is:

'You don't know how to listen.'

We accept that we might need to learn how to put our words together. We accept useful techniques on 'Speaking' such as those set out in the first three chapters.
But 'Listening' . . .

'I know how to listen. Sure I do. I pay attention. I don't need any help. So what's in the next chapter? . . .'

Wait! Very much of our listening is ineffective, as we shall see. People half-listen, or even less than half-listen, for much of the time.

Man at party: 'I'd like to build on my plot, but I don't have the money.'

Builder friend: 'I'll be round to see you in the morning.'

The builder only half-listened. He heard the positive part. 'I'd like to build.' He cut off the negative, 'Got no money.'

This sort of conversation happens very often. We hear only what we want to hear.

■ **Good listening is important to you.**
■ **The better you listen the better you *participate*.**
■ **The better you participate the more you can *profit*.**

This chapter is about some techniques which you can use to improve your standard of listening.

☆ The factors that can interfere with your effective listening will be explained.

☆ We will discuss how easy it is to learn to listen better.

Also, as a bonus, there is a section on reading, which is another form of input, the effectiveness of which can often be very much improved.

And there is something on 'Telephone Tyranny', which is what can happen to us much of the time, on our incoming calls . . .

Listening . . .

Those who speak, sow . . .
Those who listen, reap . . .

You spend so much of your time in listening, much more than you do in speaking. You continually find yourself as a part of a group, all listening. While your own turn to speak comes around less often.

Each year I ask students:

'What can we do to improve our listening?'

And the answers are nearly always the same:

1. The speaker must talk louder.
2. The speaker's voice must not be monotonous.
3. The speaker must have something interesting to say.

You see the viewpoint? It is not our fault if the message fails to come across. Blame it on the speaker. And quite true, of course. Many speakers *are* hard work to listen to. Which is all the more reason for we listeners to need to learn how.

⇨ The speaker who *is* easy on the ear is that rare delight, the listener's speaker. Who does consider us poor listeners by:

☆ Speaking to be heard

☆ With a voice which shows enthusiasm

☆ And with something worthwhile to say

We will come back to how to be a good listener's speaker, further along. First, the more usual speaker:

> Speaking inaudibly . . .
> Speaking monotonously . . .
> Speaking with nothing interesting to say . . .

This 'speaking' does not have to be done by somebody standing on a platform. There are many other occasions during the course of the day when you have to listen. There are discussions across a desk, there are meetings, there is general conversation.

It is not quite so easy for a speaker to be inaudible when speaking to such smaller groups, although this can happen as we will see. 'Monotonous voice' and 'dreary subject' are unfortunately frequent wherever a mouth can be opened. In every speaking situation a subject under discussion can be treated with such dreariness and opaqueness that it congeals.

There are three main reasons for lack of clarity:

1. The speaker has not prepared.
2. The speaker is too lazy to explain.
3. The speaker does not know what he or she is talking about.

You will be able to recall many actual examples . . . Sometimes you can ask for, 'One more time please. And please speak up. And please explain logically.'

But when the person speaking so poorly is a customer, or your MD, it will not be politic for you to be so blunt. You will have to make up for their bad job of talking with your own extra-good listening.

■ **The worse the speaker, the better you have to listen.**

Now we move on to what you can do practically to improve your standard of listening. With first an explanation of the basic problem.

Remember the diagram in Chapter 2? The one which illustrates 'The Perilous Path'? Which shows how your many teeming thoughts have to be funnelled into a very few words?

This next diagram shows another view further along the same path, at the point where spoken words are turned back into thoughts.

The Perilous Path — 2

Few words again, let loose among many teeming thoughts.

For our brain works fast. It does not need long to process the words we hear. How long? Average speech is at the rate of 120 words a minute. While when we read we can understand every word, easily, at *four times that speed*. We can process words very much faster than any speaker is able to produce them.

The block diagram illustrates this fact. There is the one-to-four ratio. 'Listening time' needs to be only a quarter of 'Speaking time'.

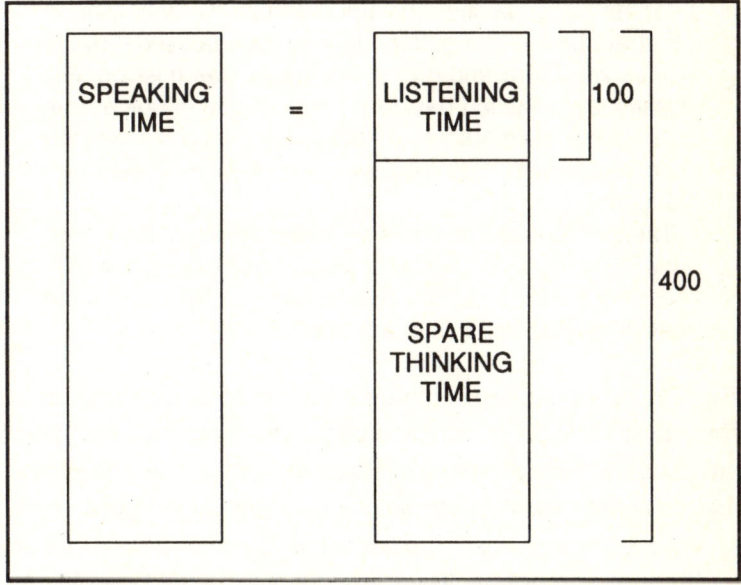

There is plenty of 'Spare thinking time' left over.

It is this spare time that is the problem. What we do with this unused but available time decides how well we listen!

We can occupy the spare time in three ways:

— in Emotional pre-occupation
— in Mind Wandering
— or by Better Understanding of the Message

With the first two being obviously negative and non-productive.
So how to eliminate them?

Emotional Pre-occupation

> We were going to the movies one evening, my wife and I.
> We had to park a short distance away. As we walked around
> a corner we came suddenly upon an elderly man, lying in
> the street beside the gutter. He was well-dressed, but his
> clothes were torn and one of his shoes was missing. His
> glasses lay smashed beside his face. Blood dribbled from
> the corner of his mouth. He had been hit by a car. A woman
> knelt beside him. She was weeping. A small crowd had
> gathered.
>   Then an ambulance could be heard approaching. I took
> my wife by the arm. 'Come, he will be well looked after.'
>   I saw the movie, but followed none of it. Perhaps he had
> been coming to see this movie, too?

An extreme case. Deep churning emotions do block out all input
for quite a while. Even minor emotions can occupy a large part of
our minds, and interfere with our listening. We may hear the words
that are being spoken, but they do not register, they mean nothing.
— An argument at the breakfast table, the after-taste of which
    lingers—win or lose. Then, at work, you are told the plan for
    the day.
    'Pardon, what was that?'
— This weekend is going to be marvelous. At the beach, with my
    Special Person . . .
    'Which figures, did you say?'
— He's so old, and years out of date. What does he think he can
    teach me?

This last example is prejudice, rearing its ugly head. It is so easy to be prejudiced. About the speaker, about the subject, about anything we choose to dislike. And it is so easy to dwell upon prejudice, and brood about prejudice, and blow prejudice up out of all proportion. So that we may manage to hear a few words but be so pre-occupied with our devouring prejudice that we have no time to interpret the *message* at all.

■ **Always listen with a clear and open mind.**

So easy to say, so easy to believe in, but not always so easy to do.

Mind Wandering

> A training session. At tea-break a young man comes to me. 'Pity about all the noise of the building alterations,' he says. 'I find it difficult to concentrate on what you are saying. Some of it is quite interesting, too.'
>
> (Yes I know. Building alterations should not be going on near to where a training session is being held. But these things do happen.)
>
> 'Think of yourself at a party,' I say to him, 'where there is a loud gabble of voices. Then you meet a young blonde. She smiles at you and she speaks, quite softly. You will find yourself able to hear every word.'

Our sense of hearing is quite wonderful. it has such selectivity. We can filter out and ignore all intruding sounds. If we want to.

We have to concentrate our listening, upon the words of the speaker. We must cut off all auditory distractions. Whether annoying (noise) or pleasant. (A radio is playing somewhere. What *is* that tune?)

This is the trouble with distractions. They distract. They set us to thinking, and we quickly use up all of that available time.

— A smell of cooking.

> 'Gee, I'm hungry. What I could use now is a nice juicy steak.'

— A picture on a calendar.

'I really must get down to the coast for a break . . .

We can quickly put *all* of our mind to day-dreaming. It is so easy. And often so tempting.

Whenever I speak in public I have a good look at the venue beforehand. If there are any pictures, or promotional displays, or anything with reading on, behind my proposed speaking position, I either change this position or have the offending item moved. Clocks are bad, too. Very distracting things, clocks.

Although none of this precaution will hold back the determined mind-wanderer. The mind determined to wander can be set away upon its errant course by the glimpse of a fly on the wall.

But the removal of any large, bright, and obtrusive distractions must help.

Your mind tends to wander too, doesn't it? Everybody's does. It is so easy to think of *other* things, rather than to concentrate upon the task in hand.

Which task could well be having to listen to the smoothie from Head Office who is explaining the new way to submit monthly returns.

It is important for you to know about this. For this is how it is going to be. You will end up in a terrible muddle if you do not understand.

Which is the clue to listening with your full concentration, using all of your mind, keeping your mind firmly inside the room.

■ What is the benefit to *me*?
■ What do *I* stand to gain?

Identify the Benefit

■ When listening to anybody, on any occasion,
   first identify to yourself WHAT DO I STAND TO GAIN?

This may be:

- Knowledge useful to you.

- A guide to the Attitude you should take.

- A lead on your future Behaviour and Course of Action.

The same three 'Changes' advocated in Chapter 1!

To be called for by all speakers!

But unfortunately, many of the speakers you will have to listen to have not learned this valuable lesson. They plod on regardless, saying what *they* feel should be said, not really considering *you*.

So, to be an effective listener, you need first to identify for yourself, just what *you* stand to gain by your listening. You will seldom be told.

■ What benefit, useful to me, is being offered?

It can happen of course, and does, that *nothing* useful is being offered.

Examples:

— The lecture is a re-hash. There is nothing new. (So get up and leave.)

— The businessman, across his desk, is now on about his clever son—aged seven. ('Is that really the time? I must rush!')

— The old dear at the party has cornered you to tell you all about her hydrangeas. ('Excuse me. I must go to speak to our hostess.')

BUT BEWARE!

— The lecturer could switch to something interesting.

   —Which you would miss . . .

— The businessman could have been intending to return to 'Now, about that contract.'

—Which you would miss . . .

— The old dear *needs* you as an audience.

—It is sometimes selfish to leave.

So it is usually preferable to remain where you are, even in such time-wasting and trying circumstances.

Stick in there, smiling and apparently attentive, but thinking your own thoughts. You have in fact left, in spirit. But they will never know.

The trick is to leave just a tiny party of your mind alert. Just in case something useful should appear.

PROFIT FROM YOUR MOTIVATED LISTENING

BEWARE AGAIN!

It is a great temptation to think, 'This is boring. I am being told nothing new.'

> I have a friend who farms. There is an old herdsman there on the farm who has been herding cattle for over fifty years. Whenever they meet this old man likes to talk, and he talks on and on, and my friend smiles and says, 'Ja, Oupa, ja.' And does not listen.
>
> One day my friend was marking out a site for a new cattle kraal.
>
> 'Not a good place,' Oupa said, among a thousand words. 'Water here.'
>
> And was not heard.
>
> So my friend built his kraal, and heavy rains came, and a spring appeared, and the new kraal washed away.

Never write off a possible informant as useless. Everybody, however humble, has some secret locked in memory which could benefit you. They are quite willing to tell you these secrets. But you have to identify the benefit, listen, and take note.

Listen your best, and learn what you can, from everybody. You can even learn something from that absolutely useless after-dinner speaker, so full of himself. You can learn about speechmaking. You can learn what not to do.

There is one circumstance under which you have to leave. Leave the lecture, excuse yourself from the meeting, drift away from the conversation.

This is when you are unable to hear.

— The public address system is intolerable. (Too soft—too loud—too distorted. And nobody is making any useful effort to fix it.) Stand up. Walk out.

— The chairman of the meeting mumbles away to the person sitting next to him. So cup your hand to your ear as a hint. No improvement? Still can't hear a word? Leave.

— The woman down the table is inaudible. Leave that conversation. Join or start another.

If you cannot hear what is being said there is no point whatever in staying on, just to be polite.

Understanding the Message

Right, you have identified the benefit. 'This will help me. This I have to hear.'
So now to the next stage.

⇨ How to concentrate on the *meaning* of what is being said.
  Here is the best way I know.

■ *Consciously* and *Continually* ask yourself,
  WHAT IS THE SPEAKER SAYING?
■ Then *paraphrase* into your own words, the *essence* of the
  current piece of message. Explain to yourself THE
  SPEAKER IS SAYING THAT . . .

Example:

> SPEAKER: 'The Cape Vulture is not quite an endangered species, but numbers are falling steadily. The great flocks which I remember seeing as a boy are no longer to be found. This is partly due to a lack of carrion. Gone are the vast herds of buck, killed and picked over by carnivores, the still meaty carcasses left for the scavengers. Nor are carcasses of the domesticated animals which have replace the buck available in any quantity. The modern farmer is efficient. Few sheep perish out in the veld. The occasional cow which dies of natural causes is quickly found, examined, and buried.'

What is this speaker saying?

> The speaker is saying that the Cape Vulture is dying out because of a shortage of its natural food.

Then on to a good listen to the next portion, with a summary of the next point . . .

A technique so simple and useful that, if you remember and use only one of the skills taught in this chapter, then this is the one it should be.

It will help you to listen and to understand better. To a degree you will find remarkable.

1. **Continually ask yourself,**
   'WHAT IS THE SPEAKER SAYING?'
2. **Then put into your own words,**
   'THE SPEAKER IS SAYING THAT . . .'
3. **There is a third useful stage to add:**
   QUESTION TO UNDERSTAND.

Which does not mean leaping to your feet to shout, 'Hey, I don't quite understand! Would you say that last bit again, please?'

We can question to understand quite silently.

We can ask ourselves:

'What is the importance of this particular point?'
'How does it fit into the sequence?'
'Why is the speaker using it?'

And similar such probes. You will find yourself asking more silent questions, which will become more penetrating and more useful, as your power of listening improves. As your listening becomes more *effective*. To use up all of your available listening time.

Always try to discover the *reason* why something is being said. Then put this reason into your own words:

'We are being told the plight of the vulture in order to make us aware.'

(You will realise that there are many occasions when you *can* ask your questions out loud. At meetings, at group discussions, across a desk. This is 'Active Listening', useful hints on which will follow shortly.)

But first:

Note Taking

Some people take down copious notes, of all that is being said to them, while others take no notes at all. There seems to be no middle path.

Many students are compulsive note-takers. I find this to be quite off-putting when I lecture. I look at the tops of bent heads, I watch frenzied scribbling. What *is* all that they are writing? Are they attempting to copy down my every word? And how can they really be listening, while they scribble away non-stop?

But the taking down of notes is a personal and individual pursuit, so by all means do it your way. By all means write down the notes you feel you will need.

Although here are some good guidelines:
1. Write down your *summary* of each important point as it is made. (The Speaker is saying that . . .)
2. Note *why* the point is important.
3. Add any significant facts and figures.

Do not write down reams and reams of the *actual words* used by the speaker. Which is being quite unselective and no better than a tape recorder.

You will realise that your summary points are the Key Points of the message. In a perfect world your Key Points will exactly match the Key Points used by the speaker when preparing. This is not a perfect world. But with a reasonably competent speaker, and with you working hard, the preparation list and your list should end up pretty much the same.

To summarise:
☆ The good listener keeps a clear and attentive mind.
☆ The good listener identifies the benefit.

☆ The good listener notes the meat of the message.

The 'Listener's Speaker'

Now that you can appreciate the factors which make for effective listening, you will also realize that the good speaker can help the listener. By speaking with the *listening process always in mind the considerate speaker can promote the smooth reception of the message. Which can only be good for the speaker.*

Check-list for the considerate speaker:
— Can they all hear? (The primary responsibility).
— Am I stating the benefits? (They must be told what they stand to gain).
— Am I sharing my Key Points? (These should be summarised clearly).

It also helps when the speaker explains the *relevance* of each point. This should be more than a brief:

'There is a new company logo.'
or 'The clubhouse is to be painted bright blue.'
or 'I am going to leave my wife.'

They will understand and accept so much better if told *why*.

• Or, of course, they can be left to puzzle out the reasons for themselves.

• Which could casily be the wrong reasons . . .

• So better to tell them.

Four Levels of Attention

At the end of a certain TV show—I can't remember which—an excited voice sings out, 'Performed in front of a live audience!' This always amuses me. For there would be little point in performing in front of a dead audience. It amuses me more than the show.

Your audiences, because they are made up of people, will vary in their level of attentive listening, from the equivalent of dead to being alive and well, and these levels do not stay constant. They change. With a one person audience, a number of levels could be exhibited in turn.

I say exhibited, but that is the wrong word. You cannot see these levels, but you can *feel* them. In the individual in front of you, or collectively of a group. For audiences do maintain a coherence, they do tend to respond as a mass. They generate 'shared feeling', vibes which you can detect.

There is a calm about an audience that is with you, a restlessness about an audience you have lost. Although there is not a great deal you can do about a lost audience—after you have lost them. But you can do something in advance to prevent them from drifting away. *You can make yourself easy to listen to.*

So, whenever you have to speak, think of the four levels about to be described. Every member of your audience will be moving from one to another of them, all the time. Make it easier for them to move—upwards! Up to number one!

We start with a look at the lowest level:

4. The 'Jeremy Benthams'

Jeremy Bentham was a child prodigy, born in 1748. He studied law, made money, travelled widely, then gained some fame as writer and philosopher.

After a long and eventful life, spent alone for he never married, he became enwrapped in a dark melancholia. In this state he added a condition to the bequest of his considerable wealth to the University College Hospital in London, of which he was Chairman of the Board. It was a bizarre condition. He was to continue to sit on the board. His skeleton, dressed in his clothes, was to be placed in a chair at the table, with his skull in a glass case between the feet. A wax mask of his features was to be set upon a wooden head.

Jeremy Bentham died in 1832. His macabre request was carried out. He continued to sit at meetings, to be recorded as 'Present, but not participating.'

You will find many 'Jeremy Benthams' in your audiences today. They sit there, silent and unmoving, staring with unseeing eyes, 'Not participating'.

School teachers know how to bring the dead back to life. In times gone by they threw chalk, or even a solid hard duster. Today they shout, 'Hey you! Yes, YOU! Stand up and repeat what I said.'

In an adult training situation you can be more genteel.

'Would you like to tell back to me what I said, please? In your own words.'

When they sit in an audience which is not amenable to, or suitable for, your calls for audience participation, then the Jeremy Benthams of this world are lost to you forever. Their bodies may sit there, but they are far away in spirit. In their minds they are fishing, or designing a new sports car, or meeting a fairy godmother in the bush . . .

3. Marginal attention

At the next level, slightly higher up, are those who give you marginal attention. There are very many of these. They are easily distracted, you can even spot them looking around for distractions. They do half listen to you, but are too lazy to follow through. So they do absorb a part of the message, but miss out on the rest.

Example:

'Did you really mean what you said earlier, about sex being a strain on the heart?'
'I also said, 'After the age of eighty'.
'Oh, I missed that . . .'

All you can do is be aware of *maintaining* a high level of interest. You do this by stating and re-stating the benefits, by continually showing your own enthusiasm, and by striving to be lively and clear and concise.

2. The group that pays attention

And they try to understand, they really do. they lean forward. You can see eagerness in their eyes. But they follow your basic message and do not see beyond. They may take in the facts but they do not appreciate the implications.

You can help these eager people. You can *tell* of the wider picture, of the reasons why, of the possible effects.

It is so easy to assume that because *you* know all the ins and outs, then everybody else must know too.

Most will only know if you tell them.

1. The stars at the top!

The gems. The rare ones. They hear all your words, they gather in all you say. They appreciate the full value of your total message.

In order to enable more of your listeners to lift themselves up to join this profiting company you must first be sure that you do offer a message that *is* full and which *does* have value.

Then make sure that this message is easy for everybody to follow.

Do I need to add that when *you* are a part of an audience, that when *you* are listening, then *you* must strive for category 1!
☆ By paying full attention
☆ By listening to what is said
☆ By thinking beyond the words.

Ask yourself:

'What is the speaker getting at?'
'Why are we being told this?'
'What is behind it?'

(I am aware that this listening theory is all rather basic. There are more complex and academic studies which move into such areas as 'frame theory', 'receptive centres' and 'perceptive competence'.

You may learn about all this in a reference library. But as the basics given here have been proved to work so well, why worry?)

Active Listening

In many listening situations, when in a small informal group, in business or socially, you can ask questions as you go. You can ask for more information to clarify the message, or to round it out, or to set it into context.

This is 'Active Listening'. Questioning to Understand.

(The drawing out of information in a more planned and prepared form will be covered in a later chapter, under 'Conducting an Interview'.)

In the meantime, let us go out selling, you and I. What shall we sell today? I know, aluminum awnings. The sort that people have fitted over their windows.

This is not to be a cold call. We have been given the address of a man who sent in a coupon. And, as it happens, this being a Saturday morning, his whole family is at home. (We are keen selling people, you and I. We work on a Saturday. There are only two types of selling people. Keen, and unsuccessful.)

So now we can practice our selling skills. And our listening, as we find out what this family thinks about our wonderful product.

Knock! Knock! on the door. Here we go. The man of the house answers.

'Good morning,' we say brightly, 'We've come about your Shady Days awning.'

Silence. He stares.

This is not quite as the man back at the office said it would be. This customer does not seem to be 'Eager to buy.' He is giving out no eager 'closing signal'.

But he does motion us in. He shows us to chairs. And says not a word.

This customer is a 'Clam'. This is one of the categories of customer that we will be able to practice our Active Listening on. There are four common categories of customer and, as a matter of coincidence, the other members of this family, who we will shortly be meeting, represent the other three.

■ **Many of the best professional buyers I know are Clams. A Clam can sit behind a desk, staring, saying not a word, not responding at all. While poor visiting Salesperson spills out heart and soul and catalogues, all over the carpet. It is not easy to be a Clam. But it is a good technique to follow, a good way of listening, when you are being sold to. Take in all, give away little.**

So what do we need to hear from this man? Well, *anything* will do, as a start. We need *some* response, to guide us in our selling spiel.

So we try a standard selling technique. We ask a simple question that is easy to answer, 'What colour stripes would you like on your awnings? Green or Red?'

Quite wrong, as we shall see.

This is a practiced Clam. He smiles, very slightly, but he does not speak. He picks up one of our catalogues.

Now enters his wife. She is a Yak-Yak, a compulsive talker. She is away and going before she is even into the room. '. . . is that your car outside, the blue one? I love blue cars, but Cedric prefers orange. A blue car *says* something, I always say . . .'

We are supposed to be listening here. But not to non-stop nonsense. We want to hear about her *needs*. Listen to the customer's needs, as they concern your line of business, then show how your product can fulfil these needs. This is a basic principle of selling, we have been told.

There is only one way with a Yak-Yak. You have to interrupt. You have to stop the flow. You have to force this one to your subject.

So: 'Let's talk about awnings.'

'Awnings?' she says, 'I thought you were here about the drains.' Then off she goes again. About Cedric, about the cat, about the price of cabbages . . . 'And I always say . . .'

'Let's talk about awnings.'

It can be hard work.

Now enters daughter.

'Did I hear you discussing awnings, or something? I suppose they would be rather nice. But on the other hand . . .'

Daughter is a Ditherer.

So, for our Active Listening, what do we need to ask her? In order to hear a useful message?

We need some definite reaction. We need more than her, 'I suppose awnings would be nice.' We need to hear some decisions.

So, we lead. 'How do you cope with the heat in summer? Did you know that awnings drop the temperature in the house?'

But we must not lead too much. We want to hear what *she* thinks. Not what we tell her to think.

'So you are the people who are trying to rip us off?'

This is the Son of the house. He is a Pig.

With a Pig you have to stay cool. It is often a temptation to be rude back. Don't do this. Stay cool.

Smile. Poise pen over note-pad.

'And just what specifically do you have against us?'

Ask for *specifics*. Ask for an actual complaint. Do not be cowered by indefinite moans. You want to hear the true facts, if any.

This fixes Pigs. They do not like to be pinned down. For they seldom do have any definite objection. So they have to back off.

As this one does now. He leaves. Snorting.

Now Clam speaks, for the first time. 'I've been looking through your catalogue here,' he says, 'I've been reading the specifications. I like specifications. I'll take your "726" model, over all the front windows. Will you accept my cheque? Will my cheque do as deposit?'

Sweet words. We can get lucky.

But we could have succeeded sooner. We should have concentrated on Clam. He is the Head of the House, he makes the final decisions, he signs the cheques.

It was all very well to maintain good relationships with Yak-Yak and with Ditherer. (A good relationship with Pig is impossible.) It never does any harm to listen to people, and to ask questions, to find out what they think. But this is PR activity. It does not lead to direct results.

'So I took him to lunch and I chatted him up a bit and he seems quite interested.'
Every Sales Manager knows this story. And asks, quite understandably, 'So when do I see an order?'

Had we worked a little harder on Clam, had we asked intelligent questions in order to listen to him, in order to know him better, we could have discovered much earlier that he is a facts and figures man.

We should have asked, 'What would you like to know about our product?' Then we could have helped him more and with less overall sweat.

He might even have given us a larger order . . .

> **Listen for what you need to know.**
> **Question if they do not tell you.**
> **Listen to the right person!**

An exaggerated tale about an exaggerated family? Perhaps. But no less useful. For there are plenty of Clams, and Yak-Yaks, and Ditherers, and Pigs about, in cities and dorps all over South Africa. There are also Complainers, and Misers, and many other varied types, in the complex human mixture.

You will rub up against all of them—hard—if you sell. In fact, you will encounter all of them continually, in any walk of life. And by listening better to all these types of people, by listening to what they have to tell you, you will find yourself able to *understand* them better.

Why, they are all rather like you and I! Even Pig has his human moments.

You will realise that 'Good Listening' is not an art to be practiced in isolation on its own. It is a part of our human relationship. A part of good communication.

Common hindrances to good relationships are Argument and Persuasion, both often practiced without due forethought and skill.

Smoother and more effective Persuasion, and cooler and more effective Argument, are the subjects of the following two chapters.

But first, some hints to improve your reading.

How to 'Input from the Written Word'

Input from the written word? Why so clumsy? Why not a simple 'How to Read'?
Because we can read without taking anything in. That's why.

■ **We can hear words without listening.**
■ **We can read words without absorbing.**

The written word has so much to offer. From so many sources.

☆ The Written Word travels in Time.

☆ The Written Word travels in Space.

You can sit down, today and wherever you might be, to read the words of Joseph Addison (1672–1719).

> 'Books are the legacies that genius leaves to mankind, to be delivered down from generation to generation, as presents to those who are yet unborn.'

With one final exception, we will be discussing the reading of non-fiction, that is reference books and specialised books, which contain information that we need to know. Which we need to study.

One big advantage of reading over listening:
We can read at our own pace, in our own time.
— While the spoken word is ephemeral. Once spoken, words are gone forever. You have but one chance to hear.

One big disadvantage of reading:
The author is invisible.
— So the message is one-way, we cannot comment back. (Although some people do try, of course. They scribble their remarks in the margins of books. But the author cannot reply. Particularly if the author is dead.)
— With the spoken word there is usually some opportunity for questions and answers.

One big similarity between reading and listening
You can practice your same 'What is the message?'
1. What does the writer mean?
2. The meaning of this passage is . . .

Exactly the same technique as used when listening! At the end of each page, or at shorter intervals should the text be difficult, stop, put down the book, take up pen and paper, think, analyse, consider. Then write down your own short summary, in one sentence if possible:

The meaning of this passage is . . .

Try this right now! With this book. For the first part of this 'How to read' section you should come up with something like: 'Reading can range wider than listening and be more deliberate, but it is one-way.' Followed by, 'I can read in the same way that I listen.'

For this simple summarise-as-you-go is as easy when reading as when listening. Easier, because with reading you can take your time. You can pause as long as you like while you consider the third stage of the standard procedure:

3. Question to understand.

Ask yourself, 'What is the real point here? What is the writer getting at?'

(That, 'I can use my new listening technique to help my reading, too.')

Concentration

As we have noted, we can process words much faster as we listen than they can be spoken. Which leaves spare thinking time which has to be usefully filled.

With reading, we proceed at our own pace. We can read at the speed at which we can understand. So we can vary the pace. Faster when the subject matter is easy, slower through more difficult passages. With the opportunity to go back to re-read, should this be necessary.

During this process of reading to understand there should not be any 'spare thinking time' left over. But it can happen. Concentration can lapse, and the mind wanders. Away from the printed page,

away from the subject, out of the window and far from the room
. . . 'Gee, I can't wait for my trip to Mauritius.'

When you want to read seriously you have to concentrate upon the
subject in hand. Do this by allowing yourself frequent rests for
relaxation. Read a page, do your summary, understand. Then
stretch, and loosen your thoughts for a moment.

After which, refreshed, you can return diligently to the task in
hand.

The Power of Print

We often look a little sideways as we listen to the spoken word.
We may not always agree with all that is being said.

Yet we tend to accept every printed word as the solid truth. 'See,
they've printed it here. So it must be true.'

Not so. Writers, even more than speakers, are inclined to ride a
favourite hobby horse, grind a personal axe. They use the printed
page to further their private purpose. They twist the truth a little
here and a little there to make a favourable point.

Or some vital facts may be omitted or distorted quite uninten-
tionally. Think of some newsworthy event in which you have been
personally involved. How accurate was the report in the newspaper? With all the skill and goodwill in the world, no reporter can
ever know what actually happened as completely and as accurately
as those who were there.

Read with discretion. Examine, think, and consider. Do not allow
your judgement to be manipulated by the assumed authority of the
printed page.

Nor should you expect to profit from all that you read. All that
is written is not wisdom. And much that is wisdom may not benefit
you. Be selective. Just as you should leave a useless lecture, so
should you leave a useless book. With perhaps a quick skip-for-
ward just in case.

Nothing for you? Snap the book shut. Go to another.

Still with me? Good.

A Common Problem

'Look,' a student in a study group said to me, 'I follow what you say. I appreciate that I must work to understand what I read. But some of the books on our list are really obtuse. I read a page over and over, I search for the meaning, like you say, and it all remains clear as mud.'

'I hear you,' I told him, 'and I'll think about it. I'll come back to you.'

'Can't you tell us *now*?'

'Tomorrow.'

This is what I advised next day:

1. Do as I did, faced with this sudden problem to which I had not given much thought. Sleep on it. The subconscious is a marvelous mechanism. It is amazing how often a laid-aside problem 'comes clear'.

    So study the difficult passages as best you can. Then set them aside. Return to them later.

2. Talk over the difficult passages with others. 'Two heads are better than one' is an old proverb, but it holds true. And a group of heads is even better than two heads.

3. Read related books on the same subject. This will often yield insight.

And of course, this is a solution, not only for studying students, but also for business and professional people, searching for sense in a lot of words.

1. Sleep on it.

2. Talk it over.

3. Read related works.

'Required Reading'

In order to rise in your business or profession, or if already risen, to stay there, you need to find some opportunity for going through newly published material. Most often, this required reading has to be done out of office hours, in your own time.

Company reports, news of new products, papers, specialist journals . . . the flow never ceases.

Then there are the endless internal reports, from inside your own organisation, and these are often lengthy and confused. And there is endless correspondence . . . You manage to keep up with daily letters but it is often necessary to go back, to wade through reams of filed material, in order to find out for yourself just how it was that the present mix-up with the Potboiler Contract came about.

So much to read, so little time.

But there are shortcuts.

The driving reason, 'I have to read all this to keep myself in the overall picture', is too ambitious. You never will be able to go through and absorb it all.

Rather decide: 'I must seek out the specific material that really concerns me.'

What is needed is a guide. What is *useful* to me in all this paper? What do I *have* to read?

Fortunately, a useful indicator to content is often provided, as an index, as an abstract, or as a brief summary.

Except in the case of back correspondence. There is no index to that.

But why not? What better task for a trainee?

'Here, take this file. Go through each letter. Mark up and list all references to the Potboiler Contract.'

This will involve the trainee in what has been going on. It will make the trainee think and study. And it will give you your index.

Make use of all indications of the content of your 'required reading' that you can find. This will save you time. You will read no more than you need to read.

But it can happen that an index is too vague, a summary too brief . . . In which case you will have to skim.

How to skim through long written material effectively

- First use all guides on content as far as you can.

- Then take note of all headings.

- Read passages with underlining, bold type, or other forms of emphasis.

- Pick out and examine sentences here and there.

- Scan full pages, alert for words which link to your interests.

Skimming is yet another art which you can improve with practice.

When you do find something useful, stop, re-read, study, make sure that you understand, then write out your own short summary ('The meaning of this passage is . . .')

One useful item, found, examined, and recorded, is worth more to you than the laborious reading, often with half-attention, of masses of inapplicable material.

The Battered Brain

Now for some thoughts on the reading of fiction. Story books. Some people, for their relaxation, like books full of action. Dead bodies and clues. War, blood, and Westerns . . .
I look for tranquility.

I have been reading the story of a young couple, married in Victorian England. A wonderfully calm period.

Each month it was their custom to attend the theatre. Then for days afterwards they would talk over what they had seen. They would discuss the characters, examine the plot, look for the meaning. The play became the catalyst for their sharing of experiences. Their route to personal communication. A focus for their happy lives.

We watch third-rate drama on TV and then we go to bed. We have little conversation. Why, only this morning I saw in the newspaper an advertisement for a new shape of bunny aerial. This is heralded as being a 'conversation piece'. If the people of South Africa are down to discussing bunny aerials, then we are indeed in a sorry state.

Last year, as an after-dinner speaker I said, 'All that is required of a TV production is that it has police cars flashing in the night, a helicopter chase, and plenty of orange explosions.'

I added, 'In future they will probably even dispense with the plot.'

I said this as a joke. And the audience laughed. But the all-noise minimal-plot 'show' is already here. Right now. And offering us very little to talk about.

Suggestion! Form your own private two-people-only 'Book Discussion Club'. Share a good book, with a good story to it, with somebody close to you, then talk it over together. Open up on how you really feel. How you have been affected.

You will find that there is a most wonderful benefit to be had from such reading and talking. You will really find yourself communicating.

Hey! Hold on a moment . . . Isn't all this supposed to be about how to *profit* from communication? So what's this relax-with-a-story-book-and-then-talk-it-over nonsense? Waste of time!

The *relaxed* executive, interested in people, interested in everything, enjoying conversation, is the one who stays on the ball. Have you noticed?

The Tyranny of the Telephone

I am trying to concentrate.

Chirrup! Chirrup'

'Yes!'

Why do we allow this piece of talking plastic to rule our lives?

Worse.

I go to see my insurance broker. I place my papers upon his desk.

Chirrup! Chirrup!

And of course he answers the thing.

I gather what the call is about. He is being asked what he would like to order for lunch. Which trivial matter takes automatic preference over me. And I had had the courtesy to arrange an appointment.

The man murmurs on and on, 'Yes . . . that will do . . . and what else . . .?'

I gather my papers. I stand. I walk out.

There is more than one insurance broker in this town. I do not even say goodbye.

1. The efficient executive arranges an 'open hour' for his incoming calls and lets this time be known.
2. The efficient executive has an efficient secretary who filters all of his calls. Outside of open hour, except for a real emergency, she takes messages. Or arranges a call back, if necessary. (There are very few real emergencies.)
3. The considerate caller always asks, 'Can you spare a moment? Are you free?'

Do you agree with this? Good. Now let's see how you would cope in the same situation. You are at your desk, and fairly new in a new situation. You have not yet had a chance to train your secretary, you have not yet arranged your 'open hour'.

I sit across the desk from you, I am your visitor, explaining that I would like to . . .

Chirrup! Chirrup!

'Yes,' you answer.

'Mr mumble-mumble for you.'

'Look,' he starts, 'About this letter you sent . . .'

Do you say:

'I'm afraid I'm rather tied up at the moment. With an important client.'

Wrong!

This makes Mr mumble-mumble feel that he is a less important client. So you have upset him.

Do you say:

'I'll call you back in five minutes. Right?'

Wrong!

Now I, the client in front of you, feel that I am to be chucked out in short order. So you have upset me.

Rather:

'I'm sorry. But I'm right in the middle of something. May I call you back?

That's all.

And at the same time you have avoided another trouble with the telephone. The person being called—that is, you in this example—is always caught at a disadvantage.

They have the initiative.
They have gathered together all the facts and figures of the case.
Then they phone you.

And you had been working quietly away on something entirely different . . .

You do not have to accept such a situation.

You do not have to be caught short of a reply.
* Ask for a chance.
'Let me look into the matter.'
Then arrange to call back.

My final point about the telephone concerns nuts. A perfectly normal ordinary person can go quite mad when driving a car. 'Get off the bloody road!' A perfectly normal ordinary person can go quite mad when using the telephone. 'What sort of a firm are you?'

Cars and telephones seem to turn some people into nuts.
   Do not try to argue back down the phone to a shouting nut. this will lead to more shouts and accusations. Hold the phone well away from your ear. Allow nut to rant and roar. Say nothing.
   Eventually nut will pause for breath.
   'You still there?' nut will ask.
   Say, 'Yes'.
   Then make your standard offer. 'I will look into it. May I call you back?'
   When you do call back, nut will have cooled down. Nut might even apologise. I've know it to happen.

➡ In my experience, long ranting calls on the phone, and long multi-page scrawled letters, are the marks of the 'Professional Complainer'. All such long complaints should be treated with caution. Genuine complaints come as short rational telephone calls, or as short rational letters.

You may, on occasion, encounter a genuine manic nut. Who screams on and on . . .

Do not make the mistake of replacing your phone. If you do you will get an immediate call back, 'YOU HUNG UP ON ME!!!'
   Rather talk away. Not too loudly, and about anything.
   Then, while talking, put finger on button.

Nut will never believe that you would hang up on yourself. Nut will immediately phone your switchboard to scream, 'YOU CUT ME OFF!!!'

But you have your switchboard well trained too.

'So sorry. That line has gone dead.'

★ **Realization!**

For this chapter on 'Listening'.

**The better I listen the more I will profit.
I must work at it!**

SUMMARY: The Ten Key Points of Chapter 4

1. The *better* we listen the *more* we gain.
2. Identify the benefit of the message *to you.*
3. *Discipline* yourself to pay full attention.
4. Ask yourself continually *'What is the speaker saying?'* Then reply in your own words *'The speaker is saying that . . .'*
5. Practice Active Listening. *Question to Understand.*
6. The 'Listener's Speaker' *states* benefits, *gives* Key Points, *explains* why.
7. Be a Class One listener! Pay *attention. Absorb* the message. Think *beyond* the words.
8. Reading is like listening, but you can proceed at *your own pace.*
9. Do not blindly accept all that is written. Read with *discretion.*
10. *Break free* of the tyranny of the telephone. Deal *intelligently* and decisively with incoming calls.

(You may be wondering about Jeremy Bentham. Do his grisly remains sit there still? No . . . The building, and the remnants of Jeremy, went up in a final ball of fire during World War II.

Yet Jeremy Bentham lives on! You will find many Jeremy Benthams in your audiences, even today. They will not disappear in balls of fire. They will continue to sit stolidly in front of you, staring. 'Present, but not participating'.)

EXERCISES

1. Practise the useful technique of question and answer:
   What is the speaker saying?
   The speaker is saying that . . .
   A good place to begin is in front of the TV.
   Start by summarising news items, e.g.
   Small plane missing over Drakensberg
   Pilot and two passengers on board
   Helicopter to join in search
2. Same again, more TV, but this time when somebody is being interviewed. This will be more difficult. The message will be less clear.
3. Same again with a real live speaker. More difficult still.
4. A reading test. Read the 'Byzantine Greece' passage out loud to a friend. (Second choice—read to a tape recorder.)
   Common errors to be listened for:
   — words left out
   — order of words changed
   — words so mis-pronounced that there is doubt that they have been correctly understood. (Don't worry too much about the pronunciation of proper names.)
   — punctuation ignored

Reading Exercise
BYZANTINE GREECE

The Megarite colony, protected by the 'Walls Built by God', founded by Byzas in 675 B.C. at the south eastern extremity of Thrace, was unforseeably destined—alone among so many other ancient Greek cities—to become the radiant centre of a state which was to carry on Greek tradition, cloaked under the new cultural light of Christianity. Constantine's powerful city was to remain for eleven centuries not only the unique European outpost against the incessant ambitions of the barbarians but also the great Christian citadel from which flowed all social and cultural structures and artistic expressions which made up what we now refer to as Byzantine Civilization.

The convulsions suffered by the Empire from successive barbaric attacks were felt with particular sensitivity in the Helladic area. From the 4th to the 11th Centuries A.D., raids by Goths, Huns, Vandals, Slavs, Arabs, Bulgars and Normans laid waste the long-suffering Greek territories hundreds of times while Latin rule, which in Constantinople itself managed to survive only 57 years (1204–1261 A.D.), lasted in many other parts of Greece right through to the time when the Turks finally broke Byzantium up definitely in the 15th Century.

The terrible devastation and plunder accompanied by brutal occupation by armies of the same or other religions, proved unable to curb the cultural force of the Greek spirit, which had become Christian, nor was its unity broken. On the contrary, monuments of its art bear witness to its unbroken continuity and creative course through the turbulent and difficult Middle Ages.

Highly religious, Byzantine art which was the outcome of Eastern and Hellenistic (Alexandrian) elements, found its best expression in ecclesiastical architecture. Painting and the art of mosaics, closely associated with Christian churches and the needs of worship, took the place of ancient Greek carving of reliefs. Sculpture, considered to be a reminder of pagan rites, was neglected by the pious Byzantine artists and was relegated to secondary functions and decorative purpose only, such as the capitals of columns, altar balusters, fonts, etc.

From the early Christian period (2nd–4th Centuries A.D.), persecution of Christianity forced the cultivation of an exclusively necrophiliac art (reliefs on marble sacrophagi, symbolic painted decoration of catacombs) while, on the island of Milos, there is a major communal, underground Christian cemetery which must have been started somewhere towards the close of the 2nd Century A.D., remaining in use at least until the 5th Century.

However, when by the 4th Century A.D. Christianity had established itself in Greece, the first Christian churches began to be built. Most of them followed the simple wooden-roofed basilica style, based on the Greek-Roman model, which took unchallenged precedence over all other contemporary circular, octagonal, three-apse or four-apse constructional styles because it served the needs of the new worship better. It consisted of a rectangular building with narthex, the main structure being usually divided into three aisles of two rows of columns. At its eastern extremity it had a semi-circular arch while in the larger churches of this style, there was also a colonnaded forecourt (atrium). The interior was decorated with various mosaic compositions along the upper sections of walls while the lower sections were lined with marble. A large number of churches of this period (5th and 6th Centuries A.D.) have been found during excavations on sites of ancient Greek sanctuaries (Epidaurus, Delphi, Delos, Dodoni and Olympia), in large urban centres (Athens, Corinth, Thessaloniki) as well as in lesser towns known to have flourished during the later ancient Greek period (Stolvi, Dion, Phillippi, Nikopolis, etc). Most of the basilicas were found ruined as the result of the scourge of barbaric incursions or modified by subsequent Byzantine alterations. Only Agia Paraskevi Achiropoiitos and Agios Demetrios at Thessaloniki, both basilicas now restored, can give the visitor of today, as complete monuments, an idea of the magnificence, yet simplicity, of those early Christian churches. The Roman rotunda at Thessaloniki, converted in the 5th Century A.D. into a church dedicated to St.

George, constitutes in Greece an isolated example of a peripheral church.

Attempts to combine a rectangular basilica with a large hemispherical dome found their ideal solution in the church of Agia Sofia in Constantinople (532 20A.D.), the most striking building of the period of the Emperor Justinian that served as the model for Byzantine architecture.

Since then various attempts and trial solutions led to the creation of the inscribed cruciform church subject, of course, to a number of local variations. This style prevailed during the 9th–12th Centuries and persevered with a few new elements until the fall of the Empire (1453).

In Greece, the inscribed cross style is formed by the addition at the four corners of longitudinal arched chambers and by the gradual replacement of the walls of the arms of the cross by columns and arches. The pioneer church of Skripou in Boeotia has side arms extruding beyond the corner sections and shows its origin to have been that of the Eastern or Free Syrian style.

Another characteristic of the Greek version is the interchange of horizontal belts of stone masonry with lines of brick or tile and incorporation of the sanctuary within the Eastern projection of the cross, without the addition of an apse, as was customary with churches in Constantinople.

Roofing of the church round the central dome, which usually rested upon an octagonal drum, was arranged by watershed inclines over the aisles forming the cross and simple, single inclinations over the intervening corner sections. Three-sided and more rarely two-sided arches with small columns at the arrises of the dome, arched doors, dipartite and tripartite windows, adorned the outer surface of the buildings. In addition to the cruciform church, there is in Greece the octagonal type, reflected in some of the more important monuments of the period (Dafni, Osios Loukas, Nea Moni on the island of Chios etc.). In these latter cases, the large dome covers the whole of the main church. It is set upon eight pilasters arranged in pairs at the four corners of the square which support the four large corner semi-domes and the intervening arches of the cross. Frescoes and mosaics have both symbolic and functional significance. Christ occupies the central dome with the Apostles depicted amid the windows of the drum. The arch of the sanctuary is reserved for the Virgin or for the vacant throne of Christ ("Etimasia"). Scenes drawn from the Gospels and a host of Saints and holy men complete the picture which has a preordained position. From the 13th Century onwards, frescoes which provide more scope for showing movement and expression, tend to replace the more austere religious art of the mosaic. The palaeologian Renaissance (14th and 15th Centuries) found its best expression in the splendid frescoes in the churches at Mistra, seat of the Despotate of the Morea and the last of the centres of Byzantine civilization.

(With Acknowledgement to the
National Tourist Organisation of Greece)

You may have been self-conscious when reading aloud, sure. But you were also trying to be extra-careful. Can you imagine the careless mistakes you would have made if left to read this passage silently to yourself? That is, as we normally read, skipping and jumping.

5. Did you remember to concern yourself with the meaning? Did you pause to question and paraphrase? Never mind. Try this now.

    — Read each paragraph.
    — Set down the meaning of each paragraph.
    — Finally, reduce the meaning of the full passage to one sentence.

There is plenty of involved information in this piece so do not expect this to be a quick task. It could take you as long as half an hour.

5

Persuade people your way

The 'Change Business'

Whatever your occupation, business, or profession you are in the **CHANGE BUSINESS**, as we saw in Chapter 1.

In order to bring about improvements, to progress your firm, to advance yourself, to profit, to succeed, you have to initiate and bring about **CHANGE**.

To emphasise once again, there are three types of change which you can cause to happen.

☆ Change in Level of Knowledge

☆ Change in Attitude

☆ Change in Behaviour (which changes Course of Action).

You can ask for change, you can appeal for change, you can plead for change. But the decision whether or not to move always *depends upon others*. Them. The people you talk to. *They* make the final decision.

The technique which we use to encourage people to change, to our way, is *Persuasion*. This chapter is about persuasion.

A change in sequence for our opening, there.
First: The Benefit to you (You gain when you change people!)

Second: The Headline ('About persuasion!)
Which gives more emphasis to the benefit.

Persuasion and Argument

■ **Persuasion works by showing a benefit.**
Argument works by proving that *they* should agree.

So Persuasion is quieter and more friendly
—and usually works the best.
While Argument can be abrasive
—but is often unavoidable.
Nor are the two entirely separate.

■ **All Persuasion contains some Argument.**
All Argument contains some Persuasion.

PROFIT FROM YOUR EFFECTIVE PERSUASION

But you should understand the two processes separately, and should plan to use them separately.

☆ Persuade when you can

☆ Argue when you have to

> Persuasion is the carrot offered to the donkey.
> Argument is the stick used to hit or the rope used to pull.

The donkey will move for all these forms of inducement, but much prefers the carrot.

It might be thought that, provided you have the carrot of persuasion to offer, then the stick or rope of argument might never be needed. Not so. The donkey might not care for your carrot, he might prefer a turnip, or he could be feeling extra obstinate that day. You never can predict whether your wonderful carrot, the benefit you offer, will be acceptable or not. Particularly when you are selling. And we all have to sell something, all the time, as we have seen. We may not have to sell goods or services. But we will certainly find ourselves having to sell our ideas and our abilities. Continually.

Selling a Lawnmower

'You would be very happy with this electric model which runs very quietly.'
'And if I get electrocuted . . .?'

> Carrot not accepted. Benefit ignored. Persuasion didn't work. And Salesperson cannot beat Customer with Big Stick. Although many are tempted to try . . .

It runs silently, you see . . .'
'And if I get electrocuted . . .?'

> Still useless. Emphasising a rejected benefit does not make it more attractive.

'You will never need to buy petrol . . . Never loses power . . . Fewer
moving parts so lasts longer.'
'And if I get electrocuted . . .?'

> The customer has this worry about electricity.
> *Any* benefits offered, however attractive, will be rejected.
> Persuasion is useless *until this objection has been cleared
> away*.
> By using argument.
> And by **WINNING** the argument.

The response to this particular objection could be:
'Ah, you are quite right to be worried. Electricity can be dangerous.
That is why this machine is double insulated. I have seen a dem-
onstration on wet grass where the cord was purposely cut through.
The worst possible situation. All that happened was the motor
stopped.'

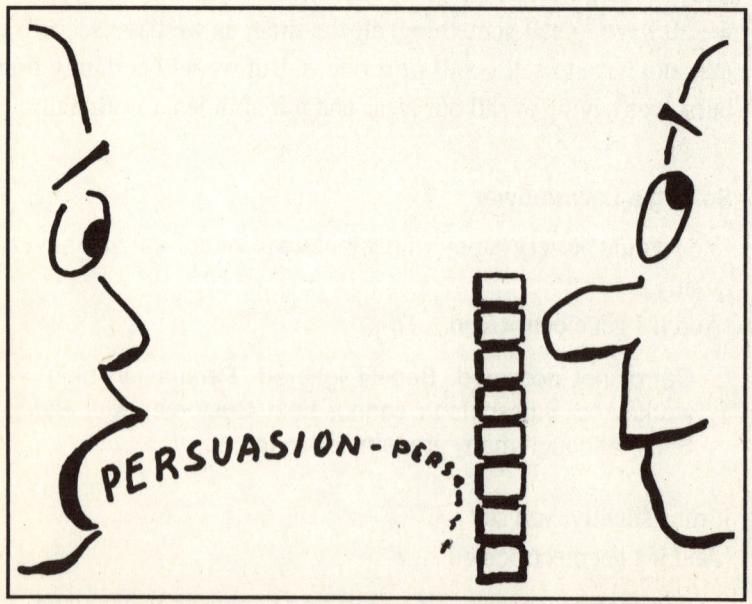

Objection builds a Brick Wall against Persuasion

Which should be sufficient to convince. If not, then more argument will have to be put forward until the customer *is* convinced.

Persuasion is never acceptable while objection lingers.

Effective Persuasion

'The public speaker must set forth with power and persuasion the very same topics which others discuss in tame and bloodless fashion.' (Cicero—Roman orator)

'The secret of success in life consists of knowing how to persuade people to change their minds. It is this power which makes the successful lawyer—and the successful grocer.' (Dr Frank Cane—American educator)

Both dead. But their writings live on, spanning time and space, as we noted in the previous chapter. We are persuaded today by their wise words. We are persuaded to persuade. Both messages offer the same strong benefit:

'Speak with persuasion and you will know success.'

But how? How to persuade?

By pointing out a benefit. That is the simple basic.

People are so selfish! They ask themselves, 'What do I stand to gain? How would this help me?'

■ So the benefit you offer must benefit
   whoever you seek to persuade.
■ Or they will see no reason to change.

Benefits can Vary

Do not assume that the benefits which you need to offer have to be real or material benefits. Like money. Although a more cash-in-your-hand benefit is easily understood. 'Save!' is one of the most common persuasions used in selling. Although not the best.

Benefits offered can be abstract:

> 'Change your level of knowledge' (and benefit by being thought clever).
> 'Change your attitude' (and feel morally good over your new decision).
> 'Change your line of behaviour' (and be seen as a person of action).

However, any benefit to which you choose to draw attention in order to persuade people to change should:

—be applicable
—be desirable
—be possible

Very often, you will need to offer a number of benefits to aid one point of persuasion. So your choice may take time, and it will need careful thought.

⇨ Active persuasion needs thought and preparation.

Just for You . . .

The more *personal* the benefit you proffer, the more it affects people *personally*, the more likely it is to appeal. And succeed. People appreciate what they themselves, as individuals, stand to gain. We are all basically self-centred.
Example:

> 'Meet me at one and I'll take you to lunch.'
> (There is often a touch of bribery in good persuasion.)

The smaller your audience, the simpler your task. The ideal being the audience of one. It is usually easy to find a benefit that will appeal to one particular person.

Finding a common benefit which will appeal to a group is more difficult. But it can often be done.

Or you can target benefits one by one, to each member of a group. Provided that it is not too large a group.

'So this is the plan for changing round the office. Jill, you will gain, with better light. Marie, you will be closer to the filing cabinets. And Geraldine, you will have more space.'

It is not impossible to persuade a very large audience. To make them think, or believe, or act, in the way called for. A skilled speaker can do this, with rousing words, with appeals to the emotions, and with cries for unity. But it is often a mob reaction. It is unlikely to be permanent.

Each individual thinks it over next day:

'He had me all worked up there. I stood and shouted my support. But vote for him? He can forget it.'

■ **There are exercises at the end of this chapter.
You must do all of these.**   **(An order)**

■ **To gain the very best from this chapter,
may I suggest that you try the exercises?**   **(A suggestion)**

Same benefit. 'Improve yourself by doing the exercises.'

But which persuades you the most? The order or the suggestion?

An effective point of persuasion is not an order, it is a *suggestion*.

'Closed' and 'Open' Minds

The effects of suggestion can vary. For suggestion is subjective, with a different effect upon each individual you talk to. So the same suggestion can lead to varied results. Some people will be quite open to your suggestion, while others will be closed.

To put some sort of a figure to it, and which I have found to be reasonably accurate:

In any audience at any one time:

> 80% are likely to be **OPEN** to your suggestions;
> 20% are likely to be **CLOSED**.

You will not be able to convert those with the closed minds. They will not accept your suggestions, they will not move to your persuasion, however hard you try. They will sit glowering. So best forget about them. Look at the happier faces. Talk towards these. There are more than enough to make it all worthwhile.

An audience of one is likely to be:

> **OPEN** to your suggestions for 80% of the time;
> **CLOSED** off for the other 20%.

The MD closed off to your wonderful new idea? Try again on Thursday.

Also!

Some of those with the open minds are likely to be not only open, not only receptive, but **EAGER** for new ideas. These wonderful people have the **QUESTING** minds. Unfortunately, there are far too few of them.

To revise our estimate:

In any audience at any one time

> 10 % are likely to have open and **QUESTING** minds;
> 70 % are likely to have merely open minds;
> 20 % are likely to be closed.

While the big boss is only likely to be really receptive for only a short period of time each working week. The trick being to determine when this is.

Three Stories concerning Beer and Persuasion

1. I am in London late in the evening after a long day of meetings. I leave my hotel for a walk to refresh. I feel like a Guinness.

Ah, here's a pub. I go in.

'What's it to be, Guv?'

'Guinness, please.'

'Nah, you don't want a Guinness so late, mate. It would sit heavy. What you need is a nice glass of our special light draught.'

But my mind has been made up. I want my Guinness! My mind is closed. No suggestion of his will change me. In fact, the more he tries to persuade, the more closed I become.

Then the barman makes a winning move. 'How about a nice draught on the house then? And I'll take one with you.'

Closed minds can sometimes be opened, with a strong enough suggestion of a good enough benefit.

2. My wife and I are walking in Paris. It is Springtime. Life can be wonderful.

'Feel like a beer?' I ask.

We pause at a cafe and perch upon tiny chairs at a tiny table. I call for two beers.

The glasses that are brought brim with Stella Artois, that champagne of beers. Very, very good. And expensive.

But this is a marvellous day in a marvellous city. We do not mind the expense.

This sparkling brew suits our mood exactly. We were open to this good suggestion.

3. I am in Cologne. I have driven long on the Autobahn with one pull-off for a snack, where I was given over-ripe sausage and under-ripe cabbage. My state of health is not the best. I check into an hotel, then go down to the bar.

'What can you suggest?' I ask the barman, 'that will really refresh.'

He suggests a cold beer, then runs through a list of brands, telling me something of each.

Kulsch sounds good. I settle for Kulsch.

Neither open nor closed, I had been *Questing*. I had stated my problem, then listened to suggestions.

It pays to Quest. To seek out alternatives. To ask questions and to listen to replies, particularly of experts. But not to be pushed or led. The Questing mind makes its own decisions.

Mmm. That Kulsch was *good*. I remember it well.

Three More Stories about Beer and Persuasion

You can take part in these next examples. Hop the counter and take your place behind the bar. And take note of the call from the hotel manager: 'Push Amstel tonight. I want you to push Amstel.'

1. Your first customer. Rather a *large* young man. Open-air type. Could be a farmer. Certainly not a ballet dancer.
    'Lion!' he thunders, bringing down his fist. This man would not even consider a Castle. Let alone an Amstel.
    'Hurry!' he bellows. 'Where's my **LION**?'
    With so closed a mind you cannot possibly win. All your suggestions, all your attempts at persuasion, would be swept aside. So there is no point in trying.

Next customer:

2. An Australian. A 'Strine. Wide open face. Wide open nature. He speaks: 'Gimme a canny.'
    'Sorry, no cannies. We serve in the glass.'
    'Oy,' he says, 'Classy! Beer in a glass, then.'
    He is quite open to any beer that is wet. He downs it in one gulp. 'Gimme another.'

Next!

3. An American
    'Pleased to have you meet me,' he grins. 'Tell me all about your Saath Aafrican beers. What's good around here?'

A gen-u-ine questing mind. Willing to accept your suggestion. Needing little persuasion to try Amstel.

Three Notes about the Questing Mind

1. Poor salespeople are impatient with questing minds. Poor salespeople think that people with questing minds ask too many questions. Poor salespeople think that answering questions takes up too much time. That is why poor salespeople stay poor. Good salespeople appreciate questing minds. Good salespeople do not mind the time spent. Good salespeople know that the 'fussy' customers, once persuaded, stay persuaded. They stay sold.
Better, once such people are convinced of the benefits of a product, they go out and *they tell their friends*. They sell for you.
2. Never ever take advantage of the questing mind by palming off a lame duck. That duck will come back to roost on you.
3. Keep your own mind, not only open, but QUESTING. Particularly when you are being sold to. (A product, or a service, or an idea.) This may take conscious effort. You may have to fight habit, lethargy, and prejudice. It is so easy to accept. It is more difficult to question.
   * Do not be too easily persuaded
   * Do not agree too easily to suggestion
   * *You* are the one to gain from your caution and care.

Some Lessons to be Learned from Advertising

Modern advertising is Persuasion in Action.

'For whiter teeth use White-O'

There is the offer of personal benefit ('For whiter teeth')
There is the suggestion of change. ('Use White-O')

The techniques of persuasion used so repeatedly in advertising must work. Or so much money would not be spent on them.

So what can we learn from advertising persuasion?

- Emotions are stronger than facts.
  Statement of fact:
  'White-O is made of finely-ground chalk, blended with gly-cerine and synthetically flavoured.'
  —Which may well be true, but so what?
  Appeal to Emotion:
  'White-O will make you feel Great!'
  —Which is evocative, even though indefinite.

- Suggestion in advertising is often indefinite.
  Suggesting a desirable imagine.
  'The younger, fitter, you . . .'
  Suggesting an attractive idea.
  'Be popular and desirable . . .'
  —Which suggestions may be short of a factual foundation, perhaps.
  But they are no less effective.
  Our pursuit of our dreams can be a powerful motive to change!

- *Emotion* can be used to drive home the point.
  Not: 'Please give for the poor of our city.'
  But: 'Little children, living in your city, go to bed hungry.'

- Over and over and over (and over) again . . .
  Kids never take in anything the first time.
  Ask any teacher. Ask any mother.
  Nor do we improve much as we grow older.

All speakers need to repeat their message. To make sure that it is heard. To hope that it is understood.

But not repeated as do advertisers.

'White-O! White-O! White-O!'

The name is hammered into our brain at every opportunity.

On TV, over the radio, in print . . . 'White-O! White-O!' Over and over and over. Until we are sick of the sound of the word. Which is why they do it, of course. Research has indicated that we remember better when annoyed. We forget the annoyance but we remember the name. White-O.

Also, to be fair, each advertiser has our attention for so short a time. A few seconds at most. (Although on TV it may seem for ever.) In that short time the main point of the message must be imprinted. Which is the name of the product. White-O.

Housewife in supermarket. Looking for toothpaste. Ah, there's White-O, she's heard of that. Can't remember much about it, good or bad or whatever, but she has heard of it. Hand shoots out to grab in an automatic movement.

When she cleans her teeth that night all her teeth fall out.

Next morning she dashes to the manager of the store to complain bitterly—or as bitterly as she is able with no teeth. Gently he tells her that the White-O she bought is for cleaning grime off the top of electric stoves.

She remembered the right name, but at the wrong shelf.

When you have a message to tell, by all means hammer home and repeat your proposal.

But do make sure that all members of your audience do also appreciate the *implications*.

The Weakness of Slogans

'We must support our club.'

'Our firm is dedicated to efficiency.'

'Let us move forward together.'

It is so easy to sell slogans. By repetition. And by more repetition. And so easy to push them into people's memories, from being heard so often.

Slogans can serve to *remind* people of what they should be 'bearing in mind'. But slogans do not *persuade*. Slogans do not cause *change*.

The teaching of slogans cannot do the job of a full statement of benefits.

⇨ What to do

When you speak, you have more time than the advertisers. Persuade with the full story.

⇨ What not to do

'You should exercise more or you'll get fat.'
'You should exercise more or you'll get fat.'
'You should exercise more or you'll get fat.'

It *is* possible to persuade by constant repetition of the same message.
The response is in desperation.
The process is called nagging.
It is not recommended.
Any move made in desperation is so easily reversed . . .

Conditioning

When you are subject to excessive repetition of a call to change, this is *external conditioning*.

But repetition does not alter or improve the benefit.
So do not accept persuasion merely because it is repeated.
Your inertia to change is *internal conditioning*.
Do not reject any persuasion merely because it seems strange or new.

Ask: 'How would I benefit?'

Think well. Consider.

Every day people lose out by resisting change.

Mission Accomplished

It is easy to persuade people to the point of their smile and a promise.

But a promise is not enough . . .

You will have to following through:

> Until the pupil is sure of the lesson
>
> Until the change in attitude has been proved sincere
>
> Until the called-for-task has been carried out.

Only then can you relax.

I never said that persuasion is easy.

However, there is compensation for your efforts.

 **Realization**

> **Whoever can persuade is a winner.**
> **I must learn to persuade.**

SUMMARY: The Ten Key Points of Chapter 5.

1. Use Persuasion to bring about Smooth *Change*.
2. *Persuade* when you can, argue when you have to.
3. Persuade by showing the *personal benefit* to be gained from making the change you suggest.
4. Choose benefits which are *applicable*, *desirable*, and *possible*.
5. Your persuasion cannot proceed while there is *argument unresolved*.
6. *Ignore* the 'Closed' minds. *Work* on the 'Open'. *Value* those who Quest for the full story.

7. Show yourself to be a *Questing Mind* to all who seek to persuade you.
8. *Learn* from the techniques used in advertising. Appeals to the *emotions* work stronger than facts. *Repetition* can imprint the wrong message. Slogans are no more than *reminders*.
9. *Do not accept* offered persuasion merely because it is repeated. *Do not reject* offered persuasion merely because it is new.
10. Remember that a promise to change is *not a change*.

EXERCISES

You now know the theory. Which does nothing for you until you use it in practice.

Once you use these principles of persuasion, for yourself, to promote change in *your* direction, then you will realize power.

(Which is a good example of persuasion.)

1. Persuade some member of your family, or a close friend, to learn something of communication. You could start with something like:
   'Look, I'm reading about Communication and it is helping me. It could help you too. Let me tell you something of it . . .'
2. More difficult. Persuade your immediate superior. Ask to be allowed to address a group of colleagues on 'Profit from Better Communication'. Think about benefits to offer that *your firm will gain* from your short talk to the group.
3. Revision. What is wrong with that last sentence? (Answer at the end of this chapter.)

APPENDIX:
How to Persuade a Traffic Cop not to Give you a Ticket

I am not encouraging people to get away with serious breaches of the law. But where no more than a warning is deserved, you should know how to escape.

This is a light-hearted run-through, but the basic principles hold true. You can use them to move into top spot over any form of officious official.

1. *Establish early Dominance*

   Get out of your car. Move into his personal space by standing directly in front of him, very close. (If his breath reeks of garlic, don't flinch. This is going to be worth it.)

   If he steps back, good. You step forward.

   Stare into the centre of his forehead. This is very unnerving. It will unnerve anybody.

2. *Break his routine*

   He has first to ask, 'Will you speak English or Afrikaans?'

   Reply in a mixture. Something like: 'Ek praat English maar my home language is Afrikaans.'

   Ignore his confusion. Give simple orders.

   'Speak up please.' 'Lend me your pen.'

   He has instructions to be polite.

3. *Keep talking*

   About anything. Never mention traffic regulations. Ignore his mention of this subject. Keep talking.

   Ignore his questions. Ask plenty of your own.

   Simple ones. 'What time is it?'

   Keep talking.

4. *Work on his weak areas*

   Weak Area One: Fear of crumbling authority.

   Tell him: 'I should report you for your attitude, you know.'

   Tell him: 'I know your boss, socially.'

   Weak Area Two: Fear of being shown up in court.

   Tell him: 'My hobby is law. I don't care how long I spend in court. I love it.'

   Note that you have not offered any positive benefits. But avoidance of being disciplined, and avoidance of suffering in court, are very real benefits to him.

5. *The Summons*

This may be a tough cookie, who insists on going through with it, who insists upon writing a ticket. (Which he might find a little difficult, as you are still holding on to his pen.) However, assuming your worst luck, he may be one of those who keeps a whole battery of ball-point pens, all different colours. One important rule you should know about the ticket. Once written, it cannot be torn up, *unless it is rendered illegible.* Your job is to make sure that it is rendered illegible.

'No sorry, that is my (maiden name, pen name, middle name). Cross that out.'

'No sorry, that's the wrong number. Cross that out.'

'Isn't that funny? A person can have left a place for years and then, when a person gets confused, the old address pops up. Cross that out.'

At this point he should slowly tear the document into shreds, stare at you silently, then thankfully wave you away.

If not, you have not mastered the lesson properly.

Or he has read this book . . .

Answer to Exercise 3

You should plan to give more than a short 'talk' to the group. A talk is no more than being 'about something'. Remember? From Chapter 1 . . .

You should put forward a *proposal.* To persuade them:

• To change their level of knowledge on Communication.

• To change their attitude to Communication.

• To change their behaviour, to practise what they learn.

6

Argue to win

(Including 'Negotiation')

If you are to succeed, you will have to argue.
Those who can argue, take control.
You think that argument is not important?
Let me show you that it is.
Believe me, you will have to argue.

So what is that? An example of Persuasion, or an example of
Argument?

Argument, you say? Quite right. Although there is an element of
persuasion ('If you are to succeed . . .'). But, as we have noted, all
argument does contain some persuasion.

This example is not only argument, it is classic argument. There
is a logical development of reasoning, in the standard form of
debate.

Note the four stages:

1. 'If you are to succeed you will have to argue'
   — Which states the proposal.
2. 'Those who can argue, take control'
   — Which offers proof of the proposal.
3. 'You think that argument is not important?'
   'Let me show you that it is'

— Which is debate. A point has been raised in opposition, so
  has to be disproved.
4. 'Believe me, you will have to argue'
   — Final appeal for agreement.

Do you agree?

Oh dear. Here comes somebody who most definitely does *not*
agree.

'So listen! Who wants to debate-like, hey? I just shout 'em
down. I just shut 'em up. And I win every time. Want to make
something of it?'

Which is another way to argue entirely . . .

Me: 'Why yes, that is certainly a point of view. Why yes, I certainly
do agree. Would you mind not hitting my arm so hard. Sir, please.'

• There are two distinct types of argument.
  Reasoned Argument and *Aggressive* Argument.

Remember the example of the donkey?

• Persuasion is the carrot

• Argument is the stick or rope

The donkey prefers the carrot of persuasion, which gives him a
benefit in return for his decision to step forward. He will also stir
himself for the stick or for the rope, but for quite a different set of
reasons. The stick hurts, so he moves. The rope pulls, so he moves.

Aggressive argument is like the stick.
It *forces* us to agree.
Reasoned argument is like the rope.
It *leads* us to agree.

I quickly agreed that a reasoned debate is a waste of time. I agreed
to stop my arm from being hit. But as soon as the bully had departed
I just as rapidly un-agreed.

This is the weakness of forceful aggressive argument.

☆ The donkey moves while being hit, then stops.
☆ While a rope will continue to pull him along.

Aggressive Argument

We cannot avoid being involved in aggressive argument, which is
not necessarily physical. It can be a shouting match.

'It is, I tell you,' they say.
'It isn't,' we reply.
'IT IS!' they scream.

As a counsel of perfection, we should not respond. But it is often
a great temptation. To shout back.

'IS NOT! IS NOT! IS NOT!'

Most aggressive argument is in the one-on-one situation, one
person and you. Although a shouter can jump up in a group, such
as a committee.

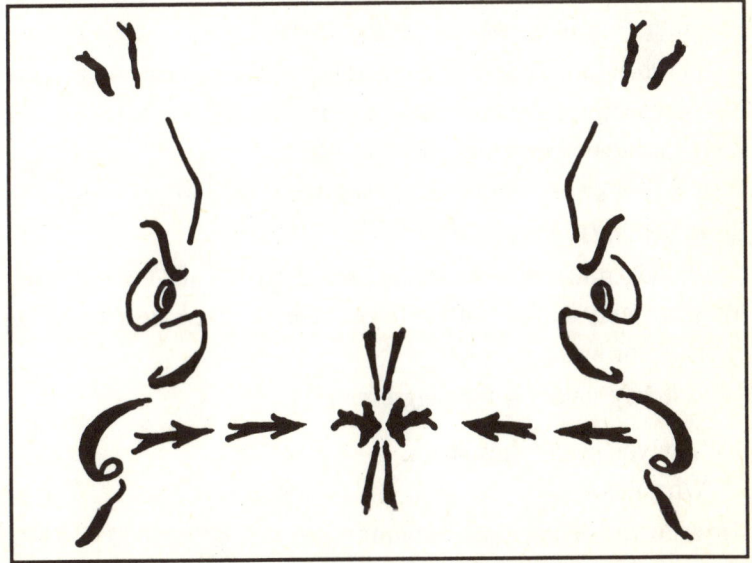

Aggressive Argument is Destructive

'LET ME PUT ALL YOU FOOLS STRAIGHT!'
(order, order.)

Aggressive argument is such an annoying disruption. Long after the verbal Kung Fu is over, people continue to fume. They resent having been shouted at. They regret having shouted. Rational discussion is impossible for quite a while.

It goes without saying that you should never ever *start* an aggro argument.

But what to do when one is started against you? How best to cool the situation?

Let us first analyze the motives of the aggressor. What is this red-faced shouter trying to gain?

Aggressive behaviour is an animal reaction. People become angry and shout when they see themselves about to lose. In order to win, they feel they have to dominate. To establish dominance by shouting (snarling) is an instinctive move.

So, when somebody who is trying to *persuade you*, then suddenly becomes aggressive, a prime cause is that the case is being lost, that you are not accepting the suggestion.

You can afford to turn away and leave shouter shouting. You have nothing to lose.

But, when *you are trying to persuade*, quietly and logically, and they suddenly realise that you have a case, that they are losing face, prestige, or whatever . . .

And they suddenly turn aggressive.

'Are you mad?' they shout.
What then?

How do you deny them this bid for dominance? How do you shut them up? Quickly and smoothly, so that your persuasion can continue?

Let us consider an actual case. You are suggesting to a colleague that the two of you swop leave-times. You offer the benefit of a quieter time of year. Less crowded roads and . . .

Suddenly colleagues gets upset. Shouts.

'You mad? Why does everybody want to push me around?'

— You could smile and walk away. 'No use talking to you while you are in this sort of mood.' Red rag to bull. 'What mood? What mood?' Colleague wants to fight. Colleague wants to prove dominance. Colleague wants to punch punch-bag. And you are taking the punch-bag away. The frustration will be worked out somehow. Against you. You will never get your leave-time swopped now.

When you want to win you cannot afford to ignore.

— You could continue with your quiet persuasion. Useless. You have not joined battle. You are not giving satisfaction. So colleague will continue to rant and roar.

And will not hear any of your words.

— You could shout back, 'Bloody rubbish, you.' Not advisable. You may win the immediate contest, you may shout the louder, but you will not win in your persuasion. Colleague will not be in a mood to concede, to change anything, after being shouted down in a screaming match. And if you should lose? If colleague succeeds in shouting *you* down? Then colleague will feel so flushed with success that the point of your persuasion will be forgotten anyway.

— You could 'Bring on the chair'. This is a circus expression. When a lion-tamer is in trouble, when a lion roars and acts aggressive, the trainer will grab a chair. He uses this to distract. He fences with the chair, pointing the four legs at the lion. It is not only the chair, but the division of attention of the four legs, that confuses the beast. Which leg to choose to paw and bite? So, loudly to gain some attention, raise diversions.

Ask: 'How is that other job going? Have you finished the

figures?'

Colleague pauses. 'What figures?'

The best points of diversion are vague.

You can divert and stop quite an aggressive attack in this way.

— However, your best course is to concede defeat. Hold up your hands. Say, 'You are quite right. You win.'

This stops colleague dead. In surprise. There is now no point in colleague going on.

So walk away. Come back to persuade later after the air has cooled down.

You will realise that much of the aggression in an aggressive argument has nothing to do with the subject in hand. The lost case was no more than the trigger. The eruption of bad mood, or of bad temper, or of anger could be due to something entirely different.

But, no matter what the cause, you will need to halt any eruption if you are to continue with your persuasion.

But think for a moment before you wade in to halt the tirade. What do *you* really stand to gain, even if they are persuaded? Would the end result really be that much advantage to you, even if they do change?

☆ Not worth the hassle? Let them shout away.

☆ You do need this change to take place? Calm them any way you can.

Viewed any way, aggressive argument is not an effective means of communication. In fact it is not communication at all.

The only situation where it seems to work is in some arguments between husband and wife. Never interfere. I did once, and was physically attacked by both for my trouble. Some couples seem to force a fight for the pleasure of making up afterwards.

Some middle-managers can be aggressive for pleasure too. The pleasure that they feel when they cut down a subordinate.

They do not make up afterwards.
And they remain middle-managers for ever . . .

PROFIT FROM YOUR REASONED ARGUMENT

Logical Argument

We have already touched upon the standard sequence for a logical, reasoned argument.
— State and define proposal
— Offer proofs
— Disprove points raised against
— Call for agreement

Mastery of this basic technique is so useful, but so seldom really thought about, that we should discuss it further.

☆ You have to prepare your arguments.

☆ Many arguments are won in their preparation. (You should *hope* to persuade without argument, but you should always prepare argument to deal with possible objections.)

Logical Argument starts with a Clear Proposal.

'What's all that noise?'
'The boys are having an argument about football.'

They cannot argue *about* something. Nothing has been put forward that can be decided upon so they will talk on and on but can reach no conclusion.

> (Committees love talking 'about' things. It is easier than debating a firm proposal. We will come to methods for firing up committees in Chapter 8.)

'Football is better than rugby.'

This is closer to a useful proposal for discussion. But all the best proposals, as we noted back in the first chapter, propose some *change.*

'More football should be taught in South African High Schools.'

Now *there* is a proposal to debate. And which can lead to a definite decision, for or against. (Probably against!)

☆ The Proposal for an argument must be *definite* and *clear*. And should propose some *change*.

☆ The Proposal must be *single*.
Not: 'More football and tennis should be taught.' Some people will agree with the promotion of the one, but not of the other. There are two distinct arguments here. They require two proposals.

☆ The Proposal must be *relevant*.
Not: 'More football should be taught because of the climate.'

☆ The Proposal must be free of *prejudice*.
Not: 'More football should be taught because it is my favourite game.'

You think that these examples are exaggerated? Show me any minute-book of any committee and I will show you motions that are equivalents.

As it happens, and it is really no coincidence, the same rules apply to a private argument as to a proposal before a committee.

Each should be precise and clear.

A Proposal of Marriage

He:	Let's talk about us.	*(Headline)*
	Will you marry me?	*(Proposal to change)*
	I can make you happy.	*(Persuasion benefit)*
She:	And what would we do for money?	*(Persuasion rejected)*
He:	Let me prove to you that	*(Proposal of a logical*
	we can come out.	*point for argument)*

Note that he has realised that he will have to argue, so he has set out the *form* of the argument. With a clear proposal.

■ **When an argument is seen to be inevitable state your proposal quickly.**
■ **You then start at an advantage.**

Clarify the Proposals of Others

Those who are not moved by your point of persuasion do not realise that by this rejection they start an argument. But they do, and it is often an indefinite argument, with no clear proposal.

You cannot argue effectively off an indefinite base. To help you to turn and convince your way, to make the argument yours and to win, you need first to state a firm and clear proposal *for them*.
In a selling situation:

'I'm not sure . . . if I do want to buy just yet . . .'
You: 'So you are saying that now is not the time?'

And even if they do come up with some sort of vague and negative proposal:

'This is perhaps not such a good time to buy.'

Turn this to a clear positive, your way:

'Let me prove to you that now is the time.'

Once again:

Never use an opposing proposal, negative or positive, clear or confused, as the basis for your own argument.

- ■ **Propose your own definite positive.**
- ■ **State what you intend to prove.**

When you are speaking to a large audience it is unlikely that one person will jump up to proclaim, 'We reject your persuasion. We propose to argue against you along these lines . . .'

You will have to sense the overall rejection. You will have to be aware of the possible reason. (Which you will have considered and thought about beforehand.)

You may then state for them their negative proposal:

'You may be thinking that this is not a good idea.'

Immediately turning this to your positive:

'Let me prove to you that it is.'

When You are Down on the Floor

There is also the situation where *you* are a part of an audience, and somebody is trying to persuade *you*. And you do not accept.

You cannot very well jump up to cry, 'I object! Prove that to me.'

But you can form your objection into a clear proposal in your mind.

'There will be a smell from the new factory.'

Then wait for the speaker to prove this point wrong.

With a clear idea of your objection, you will not be sweet-talked into acceptance of the speaker's persuasion, until you are quite satisfied that your defined worry has been proved to be unfounded.

When you are one of a small group, or are one-to-one across a desk, you can hold up your hand:

'Wait. Prove to me that there are no hidden charges.'

Force this proof to your satisfaction. Before you listen to any further persuasion.

Sequence

Now consider this:

'Believe me.
I know what I am talking about.
Change to my way of thinking.'

Back to front!

The proposal must always be *first*.

'Change to my way of thinking   (Proposal)
I know what I am talking about   (Proof of Proposal)
Believe me.'   (Call for Agreement)

That is the way it should go!

Yet we are often harangued *with the call for agreement alone*!

'I call for your support.'

or

'Buy my bananas.'

How can anyone expect us to change before they have proved to us why?

This is empty persuasion with no benefit.

And empty argument with no proof.

Proof of the Proposal

There are two broad types of argument.

1. Arguments about *facts*.

   ('This is a very old building you are trying to sell to me.')

   The best proof is by demonstration:

   'See the state of the brickwork.'

   A printed reference can also be useful.

'Here it is mentioned in this book on early Johannesburg.'
Written references are usually difficult to dispute:
'This report by the building inspector is quite definite.'
or
'Here it says in your own handwriting.'
Both demonstration and solid references are irrefutable evidence. They settle arguments quickly.

In any factual argument, however strong your case, do try to talk about the *effects of the facts upon people*.

'This building must be cold and damp to work in.'

Which makes the truth ring home.

2. Arguments about *beliefs*.
   ('The interest rate will go up next year.')

Beliefs are so indefinite . . . Many beliefs concern future events. People cling to their pet beliefs, not always logically. Proving and winning an argument based upon beliefs is seldom easy.

Beliefs are best proved by quoting an authority. Again, the printed word is strong.

'The Standard Bank Review says that interest rates are set to rise. See, here are the figures and projections.'

- The Authority you quote must be competent: (Not a doctor of divinity writing about warts.)

- The Authority you quote must be known: (Not some obscure professor from Brazil.)

- The Authority you quote must be an Authority: (Not a disc jockey discussing Mozart.)

It is difficult for your opponent in an argument to set up their own personal opinion against the views of a respected authority.

(Another form of argument which can be raised against you starts
with 'You should . . .' Win this by examining the consequences of
'if I did'. Show these to be not good.)

In any reasoned argument, never overlook the value of the ancient
Art of Reasoning.

Composite example:

Dad: 'So you propose to leave home to go into a flat?'

Daughter: 'Yes.'

Reasoning by *Induction*:

(Pine burns, Oak burns, so all wood must burn.)

> 'Look, you didn't come out at University, you don't come out
> at home, you wouldn't come out in a flat.'

Reasoning by *Deduction*:

(All men are mortal. Socrates is a man. So Socrates is mortal.)

> 'All men are after one thing. Your Peter is a man. He wants
> you in a flat.'

Reasoning by *Analogy*:

(Simpler, parallel comparison, more easily understood.)

> 'You make a mess of your one room. Think of the mess in
> a flat.'

Reasoning by *Effect of Cause*:

(Fresh footprints! Somebody has been here.)

> 'You've been put up to this. Probably by Peter.'

Reasoning by *Cause to Effect*:

('The Child is Father to the Man'.)

> 'You modern young people! Full of ingratitude!'

Reasoning by *Exclusion*:

(Sherlock Holmes: 'Exclude the impossible, and whatever remains, however, improbable, must be true.')

> 'You don't get these mad ideas from my side of the family, that's for sure. You must take after Aunt Maud.'

> 'So you'd rather I didn't go, then?'

Argument by reasoning is hard work! As is any form of logical argument, for that matter. But it can be made easier by careful preparation. Off-the-cuff argument is seldom successful.

Prepare your argument as thoroughly as you can.

> Salesperson: 'How could I have prepared? How was I to know that the silly fool would bring up the matter of colour-fastness?'

> Sales Manager: 'Always go prepared for the objections.'

⇨ The successful salesperson has thought of all objections which could be raised, and has arguments, and proofs, at the ready to counter them.

At all times, in any argument:

☆ Remain flexible

However well you are prepared, the other person can so easily alter the course of the argument. Do not labour a point that has lost its significance. Move on to a stronger point with more relevance.

☆ Go all out to win.

A logical argument is a contest. You either win . . . or you lose.

Don't forget the **BLOCKBUSTER**!

Try not to merely nibble away by stating one little point after another.

Look for a **BLOCKBUSTER**! One **BIG** Positive.

Hit them with it!

'Let me show you how this move can make you a lot of
money.'

Disprove Every Point Raised Against

Those who argue against you have a great attachment to the points
which *they* raise. However insignificant or unimportant these may
seem to you.

☆ Consider all points raised against you with due concern.
☆ Disprove these immediately.

As best you can, if not prepared for this particular turn of
argument. You cannot foresee everything. But every point
raised against you must be challenged, or you lose by default.

You may have to leave the development of your own argument,
which was going so well, to demolish a small point.

Do this. With the other person holding the initiative, with any tiny
point raised but unchallenged, you are no longer calling the tune.

Call for Agreement

Once you have disproved all points raised against you, once you
have proved all the strongest points of your own, now is the time
to close the contest.

'So you agree with me? That's good.'

And your persuasion can continue.

With, now that you are back in the driver's seat, perhaps an
armtwister:

'Let me show you one more big benefit. You cannot afford
to turn this down . . .'

The Hostile Audience

The hostile audience usually knows in advance of your line of
argument. They have made it their business to find out. They have
rejected your argument, too. True, they are wrong. They do not
know the full story, they are bitter, they are prejudiced. But they

do not like your proposals, and they are not too keen on you. How to win them over?

— Lobby. Move among them beforehand to discover who are the most critical, and just what their complaints are. It is easier to reason with one bitter individual, rather than try to convert a bitter crowd. At best, you will convince some of those you speak to, one by one. At worst, you will know the line of resistance in advance, so that you will be able to adapt and strengthen your argument.

— Seek out the friendlier ones, who are not so critical. Now you will have one or two faces out there you can smile to. And who may smile back. Having to talk to a glum audience, with hardly a recognised face or a half-smile among the long of them, can be tough. (If you find no friends, then perhaps you can plant some?)

— Start softly, with a gentle argument.

'What a lovely fine day it is today.'

Who can argue about that? So open the shutters to early accord. Do not slam them closed with, 'We are here today to talk about the increase that you are not going to get.'

— Be clear and decisive. Your uncertainty could be a target in itself.

— Be bold. Do not waver, or avoid the issue. Boldness is respected.

— Speak of 'we' and 'our' and 'us'. Too much of 'Me' and 'You' and the speaker is polarised away from the audience.

— Keep smiling.

Negotiation

For Negotiation, you need all the skills of Argument. Plus some more.

☆ You have to argue logically.

☆ You have to respond to argument logically.

☆ You have to keep your cool.

Negotiation . . .

What image does the mention of the word bring to your mind?

Tough talk across a table, laden with ashtrays, water jugs and glasses? Tough talk between Union and Management? Tough talk about wages?

Negotiation has a much wider application than that. And negotiation can be gentle.

— You may need to negotiate for more time to finish a job.
— You may need to negotiate to set up a change of staff.
— You may need to negotiate a loan.

Why, a child can negotiate for more pocket money. ('And then I'll clean my room. Every day. Promise I will.')

This is the essence of negotiation. It is a trade-off. 'If you will give me that, then I will give you this.'

A Feeling for Negotiation

Suppose you have been assigned to represent your firm in a difficult piece of negotiation. You have been chosen for your knowledge of the matter in hand, rather than your experience in negotiating, which is actually not all that much.

You realise that you urgently need to learn from first principles, so you read a book on 'How to be an Ace Negotiator'.

By realising that you need to study the subject, that it is not all bluff and bluster, that there are skills to be learned, you show that you have some feeling for the Art of Negotiation. With application, practice, learning from mistakes, and some more practice, you should eventually do well.

But, if you believe that you can become an 'Instant Ace' by reading one book, then your feeling for the subject is less secure.

And if you should feel it necessary to try to impress the opposition by placing your book prominently on the table in front of you, then you have no feeling for negotiation at all!

☆ Negotiation is not Space Invaders. Zapping your opponents, or even thinking of them as opponents, is counter-productive.

☆ Negotiation is not a game of poker. Bluff and counter-bluff do not make for useful open discussion.

☆ Negotiation is more like chess. You need to plan, consider, and be alert for opportunities. And you may need to make sacrifices in order to advance.

No—perhaps 'sacrifices' is not the best word. 'Concessions' is better. The successful negotiator knows when to pull back, when to concede.

And not to concede defeat either. But to concede in a trade-off. Knowing exactly how much has to be given in order to gain.

■ **Being able instantly to *compare value* is a prime requisite for successful negotiation.**

■ **You need to be sure of the *value to you* of that which you are offered.**

■ **And the *value to you* of that which you may need to concede.**

Compromises are seldom satisfactory

A husband and wife living in Jo'burg discuss where to go for their holidays.

He wants to go to the Kruger Park, she wants to go down to Durbs.

A compromise solution, one week of each, is not the answer. It can only half-satisfy, at best.

Nor is it a good idea to arrive at a 'fair compromise' by deciding to go to somewhere near Carolina. This can satisfy neither.

Alternative solutions are always much better.

'So how about we go down to the Wild Coast?'
'Fine. Suits me.'

In so many negotiations both parties stand firm on their 'demands', willing to concede a little, to compromise a little, if need be.

And nobody even thinks of an acceptable alternative!

How *Not* to Negotiate

1. Decide in advance what you want.
2. Climb in to bully and bluster.
3. Do not be diverted by new ideas.
4. Moan all the way home about 'those unreasonable people'.

How *To* Negotiate

1. Make no decisions in advance.
2. Go with an open mind.
3. Maintain your sense of values.

With the final and essential stage:

4. Report back accurately.

One of the most difficult tasks of a negotiator is the explaining back to those who do not know the full story, who were not there, exactly what has been negotiated, *and why*.

Case study—in a firm which buys and sells Gizmos.

The Boss: 'Look, go over to Blanks and negotiate a better price on their Gizmos. Get them down from R100 a unit to something closer to eighty-five. Don't take above ninety. Of course, you will need to offer them something. A larger order, quicker payment . . . Do what you can.'

Boss, on delegate's return: 'Well, what did you get them at?'
'R120.'
'ARE YOU OUT OF YOUR EVER-LOVING MIND!!!'

There could be several good reasons for this seemingly disastrous arrangement.

— Blanks have a new and much improved model.

— They offer this as an exclusive.

— They will support with massive advertising.

Bottom line: All of which means higher profits.

Even this tough boss will smile once he knows the full story.

Three Hats

The successful negotiator needs three attributes:

Authority

Authorised to make decisions. People cannot negotiate if they have first to 'check back with the office'.

Quick, Analytical Mind

Able to determine without hesitation the implications and value of all offers and counter-offers.

Facile in Communication

Able to explain clearly. Able to listen. Able to talk back.

In high-level negotiation, this work is done by a team. The Boss-Person, the Fundi, and the Spokesperson. In international diplomatic negotiation this would be the Ambassador, his Adviser, and a high-ranking Secretary.

But—sent out into the alien camp all on your own—you yourself will have to serve in all three positions.

Which is not all that difficult, really.

Provided that you understand and work to the basics.

★ **Realization!**

Argument is basically about clearing away other people's objections, before I can persuade them to change to my way. I must use sensible argument more.

SUMMARY: The Ten Key Points of Chapter 6

1. *Avoid* use of Aggressive Argument.
   Fend off the Aggressive Argument of others.
2. Use *Reasoned Argument* to clear objections.
3. Start Reasoned Argument with your own *Clear Proposal*. Produce a Clear Proposal to *define* the vague arguments of others.
4. Argue logically.
   Offer proofs.
   Disprove points raised against.
   Call for agreement.
5. Prove facts by *demonstration* or by *irrefutable* evidence.
6. Prove beliefs by *quoting an authority*.
7. *Make good use* of classic lines of reasoning.
8. Remember that reasoned argument is a *contest*.
9. *Disarm* a hostile audience in advance.
10. In Negotiation
    Be sure of the *value to you* of trade-offs.
    Consider *alternatives* as well as compromises.
    Be an *Authority*, a quick *Calculator*, and a *Communicator*.

EXERCISES

1. Use a logical argument to overcome an objection to your persuasion towards change.
   Find a real objection:
   — at your work

— at a club or association meeting

— at home

to some change that you would like to put through. Work out and *write down* your proposal for argument against this objection.

Use the sequence of prove/disprove/call for agreement (for real!)

Sit down afterwards, and examine how you fared.

2. Take a situation about which you feel strongly.

   Such as:

   'Nature Conservation is necessary' (fact)

   'Animals are unhappy in zoos' (belief)

   Now prepare to argue the *opposite case*.

   Marshall your proofs

   Make use of reasoning

   Write notes

   This is an excellent exercise for forcing you to think through and think clearly.

3. Negotiation. Go to an unsuspecting colleague and ask for something outrageous.

   Such as: 'Take some of my work off me.'

   Offer something in return.

   Keep it flexible.

   Encourage bargaining.

   You may even gain.

   Whether you return your gain, or confess that you have been play-acting, is then up to you!

4. Informal debate.

   Debate! Ugh . . . Memories of boring school debates with boring rigid rules on silly boring subjects.

   This exercise is *informal* debate.

   Sit around in a group. Divide into two teams, for and against. Speak in turn. Interrupt and interject. That's part of the fun.

Suggested subjects:

'The old days were not so good' (argument of fact)

'Extra-terrestrial visitors are real' (argument of belief)

'Ghosts cannot wear clothes' (??)

In formal debate the outcome is decided by an audience show of hands, which is biased, or by a judging system which gives points for a point made, and takes points away for a point lost, which is unwieldy and unfair.

Rather appoint a referee, to take notes, analyse the issues raised, and give a decision.

Then argue over this decision . . .

7

Use more than words

Whenever you speak, the total effect which you produce is more than the message of your words. This applies whether you speak to a large group, or to a small group, or one-to-one. Although many of our examples, for clarity, will be you-to-a-group.

■ **You are judged on the *impression* you make as a person.**
■ **You are judged on your *body language*.**

Both of which are under your control.

You may also choose to support your words by showing diagrams, charts, or pictures.

These can add to your total message too.

The total resources at your command are your *Total Language*.
Made up of:

> You
> Your words and how you use them
> Your exhibits

This chapter is all about Total Language.

You will learn how to support your spoken message.

I had a sudden toothache. I phoned my dentist, to be told that he was away at a convention. I was given the name of a stand-in.

Already, as I sit here in stand-in's waiting room, I am apprehensive. How good a dentist is he? Why did he not go to the convention too? Will it hurt?

I look up at his certificates hanging on the wall. Impressive. He passed his exams. But what is the pass mark for a dentist? Perhaps he only just managed to scrape through.

Finally I pluck up the courage to ask the woman sitting there, also waiting, reading a magazine, quite calm, 'Have you been here before? What's he like?'

'Very good,' she tells me. 'I have every confidence.'

At last I am shown through. I meet the dentist. He looks very efficient. No stains on his white coat.

He speaks. His voice is pleasant. You can tell a lot from a voice . . .

'I beg your pardon,' I say. 'What was that?' I had not been listening to his words.

'So what is the trouble?' he asks again.

This episode is typical of a meeting with a stranger, and it divides into a typical three stages.

1. *Advance Impression.* What you know, or think you know, about a person before you even meet. My advance impression was negative. I was prejudiced because he was a stand-in. Without the assurance from the woman in the waiting room I might well have slunk away. Without seeing the man at all.

2. *Appearance.* I had examined him carefully. He looked to be neat and efficient so I had hastily revised my opinion and now accepted him, before he even spoke.

3. *Voice.* His voice further re-assured me. I liked the sound of it. I took my place in his chair.

And all these decisions, against and then for the man, had all been made before I had listened to a word he had said!

It is really amazing how inaccurate our early assessments of others can be. And equally amazing how confident people can be that all their assessments are true.

Right! Step to the platform, will you? Set yourself up to speak, and let us see what an audience will make of you.

Firstly, they will have formed some opinion of you before you even arrived. They will already know what they think of you, based upon your credentials and your reputation.

Your Credentials

It is quite possible that you are in a position to take on some credentials for yourself, without you even trying. If you are a member of a profession, or if you hold a respected position in a respected firm, then you adopt a certain standing. Automatically. You assume a reputation, which is not really yours, in much the same way as if you had borrowed the dentist's white coat.

Even the mere fact that you work for a firm of which people have heard gives you some stature.

As a new travelling salesperson, fresh on the circuit, you would need only to present your calling card, with the name of a known firm printed upon it, to be 'in'.

So you are known in advance for what you are. Or rather for what you stand for.

(I knew that the man was a dentist. So he would be what I expected a dentist to be.)

But what *you yourself* are is more important. The particular person, not the generality.

(Although, how good a dentist?)

People soon know you for your own deeds. Good or bad. And one isolated bad deed shows up stronger than do a number of good deeds. This is a fact of life. Unfortunate, unfair, but still true. Some people do like to judge you by your past failures.

It is even more unfortunate that their determination of 'success' and of 'failure' is so often subjective, and based upon their own limited viewpoint.

> 'This next speaker is the man who collects so much for charity.'
> 'Oh yes.' (His achievement means nothing to me.)
> 'And the one after does modern sculpture.'
> 'Oh I must listen to him. (I am such an artistic person.)

You really do have to struggle to build up a reputation that people will think well of you for!

> (Oh, dear! I will have lowered my own reputation with English Language purists with that one. I ended a sentence with a preposition. They will pounce upon my error, and mark me down as a grammar mangler to be watched for ever.)

But do not despair! It is not really important what the uninformed or biased may choose to think of you, in advance, before you even stand to speak.

Continue to produce good results and you will find that this does become known *to those who matter*.

When you do stand to speak, stand confident.

> 'Believe in yourself. This makes you feel good and look good.'

Wise words. Written by Sigmund Freud. No . . . sorry. I had my notes mixed up here. I actually took that quote from a school essay, written by a child of ten.

Do you feel those same words to be so wise? Now that you know who really wrote them?

■ The effect of words *changes* according to who uses them.
■ People think back to the *reputation* of the speaker when they consider the message.

But do stand confident. Do know that every time you speak well, with a worthwhile message, that you are slowly building up your own reputation as a successful speaker. Good results do count. Your past performance does determine your future.

Your *APPEARANCE*

Appearance is used as an instant guide to character. 'I can tell so much about a person from one quick look.' People pride themselves on this.

Much of this instant character assessment is wrong. Much of it is based upon prejudice.

Test your own prejudice level:

> You go to see a strange dentist. He has a curved spine. This will have no effect upon his skill as a dentist. But how do you feel about having your teeth fixed by a hunchback?

Appearances can be deceptive. And misleading . . . Also, most people do not look at you but at your *clothes*. They base much of their character assessment on what you are wearing. Provided that your clothing checks OK they will pass you as an OK person.

> (My new dentist dressed neatly, so I assumed that he would work neatly.)

The secret is to dress *appropriately*. Appropriate is the word. The odd-ball mode of dress invites criticism.

- The man who is to speak has mis-read his invitation. He is prominent in his dinner jacket. All of the other men are wearing lounge suits.

- The lady who is to speak on 'poise' has chosen last year's fashion in eye-shadow. Every pair of eyes in the room has noticed this.

Although—given the current informality in clothes, with almost anything being acceptable on almost any occasion, it is becoming more and more difficult to dress inappropriately.

But it can be done. Pitch up at a board meeting wearing purple sun-glasses and nobody may say a word. But they will think, 'Can this clown be taken seriously?'

Later in life and if you choose, you may set yourself up as a 'character'. Then you may wear your purple sun-glasses, and a sun-helmet for Saturday morning shopping, and people will accept such eccentricities. Indeed, they may come to expect them of you.

Although whether any wise words of even accepted 'characters' are ever taken seriously, I have my doubts . . .

Your *VOICE*

An audience may consider your credentials, and they may check your appearance, but they will take far more notice of your voice.

They are happy with a speaker with a pleasant friendly voice— unhappy when having to listen to a harsh growl. (And women can growl too.)

It is as simple as that.

A good speaking voice is an asset. Which does not mean that you should go rushing off to book Voice Production lessons . . . unless you think that your voice really is that bad.

A pleasant friendly voice can be cultivated. Smile when you speak—we have already mentioned this. Ask your friends for comment and criticism. Listen carefully to yourself on a tape recorder. ('Surely that isn't me!') Mark down and work on the areas where you can improve.

Common faults:

    Too high in pitch
    Too fast
    Too sharp and abrupt

You cannot change your personal appearance.
You can change your voice. For the better. Quite easily.

A man listens to a girl on the phone . . .
He thinks, 'She sounds wonderful. I'd love to meet her.'
—He has no clue whatever as to what she might look like.
—He has flipped to the sound of her voice . . .

Your *GRAMMER*

(Spelling is important too. That should be 'Grammar'. We will come to the written word in a later chapter.)

People always like to know how they *stand* in relation to other people. Especially when another person is telling them something.

Do not try to bluff yourself that you never think of such things. Of course you do. We all do. We all assess those who speak to us. We all want to know their standing.

So how do we measure a speaker? How do we allocate them to a level, up or down? In relation to ourselves?

The measure of a speaker's standing is not by social position.
— People may rank high but think low.
The measure of a speaker's standing is not by birth.
— People may have marvellous genes but not use them.
The measure of a speaker's standing is not by wealth.
— People may be rich in substance but poor in quality.

So what do *you* think? How do you rate a speaker's standing?

By Knowledge displayed?	Close
By Wisdom displayed?	Closer
By Education displayed?	Right!

We judge a speaker by *level of education.*

Not education on paper.
Not by degrees attained, or letters after the name.
☆ But by evidence of the educated mind in use.
(Or by evidence of the lack of it, more usually.)

We listen to a speaker, eager to spot signs of a slipped education. Not so much as never having *had* the education, but not having the brains to *make good use of it*.

The speaker makes a slip of grammar. 'Now for a more better suggestion . . ..'

And we pounce. 'See, I knew it! All that education, and not being used.'

Spotting slips in grammar is the easiest way we can assure ourselves, 'They are no better than I.'

This happens every day. People are pulled off their pedestals through making a simple slip. Most unfair. Shouldn't happen. But it does.

Million-rand contracts have been lost in this manner. So do please be careful with your grammar. You can lose so much authority if you slip.

Your *ACCENT*

Let me make one point quite clear. I am not talking about Afrikaans spoken with an English accent, or English spoken with an Afrikaans accent, or with a French accent, or with a German accent. Such accents are quite acceptable, indeed they can be attractive.

The accent you must avoid using is the common coarse 'gommy' accent, or anything drifting down towards it. Use a hint of such an accent from a platform and you lose any standing you may have very rapidly indeed.

'That can't be anybody, surely?
Speaking like that.'

Suppose my new dentist had asked me, 'Hey, ken ah fix you up then?'

I would have left him like a shot.

■ It is easy to *drop* your accent, by mingling with people who talk that way.

■ It is not so easy to *raise* your accent.

But you can do it, by taking care.

Do watch your accent! Please! For your own good.

You will remember 'My Fair Lady' and the observation of Professor Higgins, 'As soon as an Englishman opens his mouth, some other Englishman despises him.'

This is 'Snap judgement by accent.'

Professor Alan Ross wrote his 'Essay on Sociological Linguistics' on the same theme. He coined the terms 'U' (for Upper Class) and 'Non-U' (for Non-Upper Class).

He made his judgements, not only on grammar and accent, but also on word usage, which we will be coming to shortly.

Two of his British examples:

'How d'you do?' ('U')
'Pleased to meet you.' ('Non-U')
'Perfume' ('U')
'Scent' ('Non-U')

It is an interesting exercise to look for similar indicators here in South Africa. We could call our strata 'P' (for Professional Class) and 'Non-P' (for Non-Professional Class).

Here are some I have noted:

'The box' ('P')
'The teevee' ('Non-P')
'Garden' ('P')
'Yard' ('Non-P')
'Lend me a pair of scissors.' ('P')
'Borrow me a scissor.' ('Non-P')

With a little diligent search you will be able to spot many more. All snobbery, of course, but it does happen. We do judge one another by the way we speak.

Clothes do not always Make the Man

A true story:

> I had to interview two short-listed prospects for a position, I had to select one. Both men had equal qualifications but the first was a little scruffy, a little down at heel, which tied in with his story. He said that he had been down on his luck and out of work.
>
> The other was very well dressed but—there was something in his voice which turned me against him. He did not sound to be as good as he said he was for he claimed a high standard of education.
>
> I took the rougher looking man and he did well. The other ended up in jail. It turned out that he had stolen the clothes he wore that day.

As we grow old we become wiser in our judgements and more shrewd. This is one of the few compensations of growing old . . .

Another true story:

> A new foreman came to me with tears in his eyes. There had been an accident at the railway workshops. His son had been killed. 'Almost cut in two.' I pleaded with Accounts. I got him a quick advance, to pay for the funeral.
>
> Then the Paymaster came to pounce. The man had already drawn all of his wages, against another and sadder story.

Growing older, growing wise, does not ensure that we will never be caught out. There are some practiced chancers out there, using all of the skills of Total Language to impress us and to win our trust. It is their profession, they become very good at it. Yet I had been sure that those had been real tears in his eye . . .

Your *WORDS*

'Words are the tools of speech'
'Words are the currency of thought'

In order to speak successfully, which means to put your message across, you have to know how to work with words.

You use words to assemble the message you have to tell.

You need to choose and use these words with care.

Some hints:

Increase your word-power!

A common exhortation (call) is 'Learn to understand more words. And use them.'

Which is all very well. But you can reach a stage where you are using long words new to you and which you learned yesterday but which very few of your listeners understand.

If you use words that are not understood by all of your listeners then a part of your communication must fail. Not only that, your long unusual words will label you as a big-head.

All the time, people are waiting for you to make a slip. You can slip by using a low-class word. You can slip by using a pretentious word. Either way, you drop in their estimation.

So, use words that are accepted and that are in normal usage. Which is not to say that you have to stick to the same words that everybody uses every day. People *use* only about two thousand words. But they *understand* five thousand. So there are plenty of words which you may not normally use, but which you may call upon to enhance, embellish, and clarify your message. And which will be clearly understood.

⇨ A good dictionary contains half a million words, and more are being added to the English language every day. To find your way around, do not use a dictionary. Use a Thesaurus. This will help you to use the very best word for exactly what you want to say Or write.

The Rhythm of words.

> Short words hit home hard.
> This is true.
> But longer words can offer a wider understanding of your intended meaning.
> Which also is an accurate summation.
> Too much use of short words can jar.

Not only that.

Short words need to mingle with long.

There is music in the rhythm of words, short and long, each carefully selected, each in its proper place.

- By using a rhythm, a good speaker 'sounds right'.

- By varying the rhythm, a good speaker avoids monotony.

- By using rhythm to underline the message, the good speaker can become great.

If you speak naturally to a rhythm, as do the Africans, the Irish, and the Italians, then you are fortunate indeed.

Otherwise you will have to work on it.

Listen to good speakers. (In person, on radio, television.) Absorb the way in which they weave patterns with their words. Word rhythm has to be *felt*. It is not a skill to be taught.

Too many Words—And you may lose Control

You can obscure your message by trying to be too clear.

> Lawyer: 'Now tell me, did you or did you not, on the date in question, or at any time previous or subsequent to that date, say, imply, or intimate, to the defendant or to anyone else, whether friend or mere acquaintance, or in fact a stranger, that the statement imputed to you, whether just or unjust, and denied by the plaintiff, was a matter of moment or not? Answer yes or no.'

> Witness: 'Yes or no what?'

You can submerge and lose your message under a messy mass of facts and figures.

Too many facts and figures, read out slowly and expected to support, more often obscure.

They become ineffectual, time-wasting, and boring . . .

But:

☆ Emphasise a few strong facts

☆ Quote a few significant figures

And you will underline your message.

PROFIT FROM YOUR TOTAL IMAGE

When you Listen

When you are listening to any speaker, on any occasion, do assess by Total Effect, but with discretion.

Consider what you know of the speaker

Examine the appearance of the speaker

But only as far as this may affect your evaluation of the *person*, not the *message*.

Try not to be influenced too much by slips of grammar, jarring accent, or by the use of 'social strata' indicator words.

All these may not make the slightest bit of difference *to the message*.

Remember: It is the *message* that counts.

When you Speak

Your audience will not be so considerate.

* They will remember all that they have ever heard about you.

* They will be critical of your appearance.

* They will pounce upon your tiniest slip.

But, to be fair, they seldom do this maliciously. People like to know just who this is they are listening to. In order to determine who you are and where you stand, especially in relation to themselves, they will judge you, often without conscious thought.

And before they even think of listening to your message.

So—to give yourself every best chance when you speak, do think about and control your Total Language.

Good Reputation, *Appropriate* appearance, *Pleasing* voice, *Acceptable* Grammar, *Unobtrusive* accent, *Well-chosen* words.
Why risk criticism?

Body Language

Quotation:
And this *is* by Sigmund Freud!

> 'He that has eyes to see may convince himself that no mortal can keep a secret. If lips are silent then there is chatter from the fingertips. Betrayal oozes out of every pore.'

Frightening! We send out signals all the time and these can be read by those who have learned to interpret this hidden language. We hold no secrets from them. So how can we attain the same expertise, how can we learn how to read these hidden signals, so that we too may know *everything*, held back and not spoken, about all those around us?

It is not as easy as that! Fortunately. If *our* inner thoughts were to be so easily available, then we could find ourselves in some very difficult situations indeed!

The study of Body Language is not an exact science. Conclusions are reached from the study of *indicators* which show *probabilities*. It is rather like the forecasting of the weather. There are many indications as to whether it may rain or shine, and the more indications that can be noted, the more accurate the assessment of the weather pattern is likely to be. But it can still be hopelessly wrong . . .

Perhaps the most accurate of Body Language readers are the professional fortune tellers. Close observation, diligence, and the knowledge of many useful signs, enables them to be able to 'read thoughts and character' quite amazingly well. Professional confidence tricksters run them a close second. With the most assiduous of salesperson practitioners, watching hopefully for capitulation signals from customers, trailing far behind.

All the experts give themselves one big advantage. They observe one person at a time. They study this one subject closely.

☆ Rule 1: Body language works best one-on-one.

Lovers can become very adept in the giving and receiving of Body Language. A man always seems to be able to understand his one and only love, even though he may speak only Bulgarian, and she may speak only Afrikaans. Nevertheless, in any man–woman situation, the most obvious of non-verbal signals are never quite as satisfactory as her whispered 'yes'.

☆ Rule 2: The word is stronger than the sign.

In the main. There can be instances of people who bluff with a spoken lie, while they unwittingly signal the truth. But this is not usual. Most people are straightforward. Relatively few are devious.

We are now going to consider a few of the common Body Language indicators that are generally useful. Should you want to learn of more, reliable and perhaps not so reliable, may I suggest that you study a specialist book on the subject? It can become all rather involved.

We are now going to consider two *directions* of Body Language.

You to them
Them to you

And two *levels*.

Subconscious
Conscious

Which gives us four combinations.

1. *You to them—subconsciously*
   Whenever you speak to an audience you signal with your body. You 'say' much more than your words. All unknowingly.
   Also unknowingly, they are learning lots about you. Instinctively, they are reading the signals that you are sending out, by the way you use your eyes, by the movements of your hands, by the attitude of your limbs.
   —If you are nervous they will know
   —If you are worried they will know
   —If you are uncertain they will know
   —If you are insincere they will know
   All the secrets which you wanted so much to hide!

2. *You to them—consciously*
   THINK POSITIVE!
   Nervous? Nonsense! I've done this before.
   Worried? About what? not me.

Uncertain? I've never been more sure in my life.

Insincere? Please! I mean every word I say.

With this positive attitude you will *exude* self-confidence. Your hands will move, your arms will gesture, your eyes will flash. You will shout out in your body language loud and clear. No problem.

You will signal 'I am in full control' Without having to think about it.

You do have one further option to use to improve your strength of signal, should you feel this to be necessary. You can add a bit of acting. You can consciously enlarge your gestures, as an actor is taught to do.

'I appeal to you all.'—Arms spread

'To raise your standards.'—Hands lifted

There are many such gesture conventions. They can be very useful for underlining your message. Provided that they are not over-emphasised, and provided that they are not over-done.

You would need to work out such gestures and rehearse them with your speech, as an actor does.

'Word emphasis' is another useful trick. Models who slink down ramps when they show fashions are taught to respond to the compère's words.

'Smooth' and they run a hand down a silky thigh.

'Soft' and they curl their fingers.

In such ways you can consciously enhance your body language. But at the risk, if you do not take care, of not appearing so natural.

You will always remember to smile. Won't you?

3. *Them to you—subconsciously*

This is when your audience (can be one person) is sending out signals but they do not know it. And you are receiving the signals—and you do not know it. Although your sub-conscious mind does register the message.

I am getting through to them
What I say is accepted
They want to hear more

— This is the positive feeling that you will get from a satisfied
audience, without being aware that you are reading signs.

Negative signals can come across even stronger.
They are bored and they want me to stop.

— Although many speakers seem to be totally unable to detect
the silent cries of anguish . . .

4. *Them to you—consciously*

Strong as your perceptions may be of your reception by an
audience, they are no more than perceptions. It does help if you
can confirm your impressions with a reading of body language.

Positive signs:

— Leaning forwards
— Eyes directly on you
— Quiet and still

Negative signs:

— Hands over face ('blocking')
— Arms folded
— Shuffle shuffle

These particular signs are all fairly basic and they are all
reasonably reliable. But, as we have already noted, all body
language signals are indicators, not definite signposts.

So do not scream at your boss, 'You are never interested in what
I say!' just because he may fold his arms.

Visual Support

Sir David Lean challenged a group of friends to recall just one line
of dialogue from one of his famous films. None could. He then
asked who could remember a scene . . . All present instantly knew
their favourite.

We remember more of what we see than of what we hear—a truth constantly being reminded to us by the purveyors of overhead projectors.

How to Fold and Fly a Paper Aeroplane

This is a demonstration which I give to students.

First I hold up the written specification for the type of paper they should use. Then I show a small diagram of how the paper should be folded. Finally I hold up a little photo of the finished craft.

They sit bemused, as well they might. All of this is absurd.

I then take the specification, I fold it slowly step by step, and I send it winging out over their heads. *This* is the way to demonstrate. By demonstration.

Yet people do hold up sheets of paper covered with minuscule figures.

People do show tiny diagrams which nobody can see.

People do produce little photographs.

☆ Rule 1: Visual support must be *visible*

Some months ago I was a part of a seminar on Industrial Marketing. The video shown was about Supermarket Merchandising. When I asked 'Why the discrepancy?' I was told, 'Well it *is* about selling and it was loaned to us for free.'

☆ Rule 2: Visual support must *support.*

Let us run quickly through the more usual types of visual support that are available to you.

Films

There are less promotional and educational films around in this age of video, but the larger clearer picture from film does have the greater impact.

Effect: Vivid and complete. Movement, colour, sound, commentary . . .

Ease of use: Needs darkened room, special equipment, time to set up.

Adaptability: Unlikely that the subject will be treated in the exact manner you need.

Video

Effect: Not too bad close up, but with more than about twenty people many are too far from the tiny screen.

Ease of use: Less fuss than film, although the equipment is bulky.

Adaptability: Custom subjects can be home-made to suit.

But . . .

— The run button on a video camera is too easy to press.

— The tape is too cheap.

— Editing is too tricky.

'Our Personnel Manager turns them out in his spare time.'

'Oh really.'

Slides

Effect: Clear colour pictures.

Ease of use: Fair. Proper screens seem to be scarce. A pink wall is not as good.

Adaptability: Easy to edit. Fairly easy to take special pictures. Commentary may be added to suit.

For a successful slide show:

Discard any slides that are not clear.

Double check for correct sequence and right way up.

Introduce the subject before showing the first picture.

Wait . . . at each new slide. Allow the audience to absorb the picture before you speak.

Do not keep saying, 'Now this is . . .'

Do explain the reason for showing each picture.

Do not flip through *too fast*.

Nor go agonisingly *slow*.

Turn off projector at end, signal for 'lights up', move to front of audience, *summarise* the highlights.

Overhead Projector

Effect: You can get photos put on to overhead slides, and in colour. But you have to send away and it takes time and it costs money. You can go directly from a PC to an overhead projector and this is also expensive. So you are normally limited to simple writing or printing and simple graphics.

Ease of use: Needs screen and projector but room need not be dark. (And should not be.)

Adaptability: Good. Useful slides can be quickly and easily produced to tell exact message.

The suppliers of overhead projectors will gladly assist you in the mastery of a few simple techniques. Such as the advantage of moving a blanking-off card down to reveal a part of the words at a time. This prevents people from reading on ahead.

What the suppliers will not tell you is that ordinary felt markers work just as well as their expensive pens. (Use the waterproof type if you want your slides to stay permanent.)

Flip Charts

There are two types of these. The more usual version is quite large, is supported on an easel, and supplies a pad of large sheets of blank paper. You write and sketch on these with thick felt markers, then, as you finish with each sheet, you flip it over the back and out of sight. It is rather like an update on the old school blackboard.

Effect: Much like an overhead projector

Ease of use: But even easier to use.

Adaptability: Very good. Adapt as you go.

The other type of flip chart is the one I like to use, although it only works well across a desk or to a very small audience. For these applications it is superb.

Take an A-4 or similar size artist's pad. It must have a stout cover, thick pages, and be ring-bound.

It is used vertically, rings to top.

To the pages paste photographs, diagrams, key points printed out . . . Anything that you will find useful to support your message.

Set the chart on client's desk. Flip it over while you talk.

Effect: Forces attention on visuals

Ease of use: Simplicity itself

Adaptability: Very versatile

> Note to Sales Managers:
> Have ring binders professionally prepared with the figures, charts, and photographs which support your current campaign.
> Give one to each salesperson in the field.
> You then have a sporting chance that each will tell the same story.

Graphic Comparison

The chart in the illustration has been taken directly from a simple overhead slide. It sets out in graphic form all the same comparison criteria as have already been listed. (The original is in colour.)

Apparent, immediately, is that the humble desktop flip chart achieves top score.

But this is a somewhat biased conclusion. My measures were all made from the presenter's viewpoint, and the limitation of this type of flip chart to very small audiences has not been considered at all.

From the opposite viewpoint—how clear and vivid is the picture to a large audience?—the film must fill top spot.

Which shows how versatile such charts can be. And how open to bias.

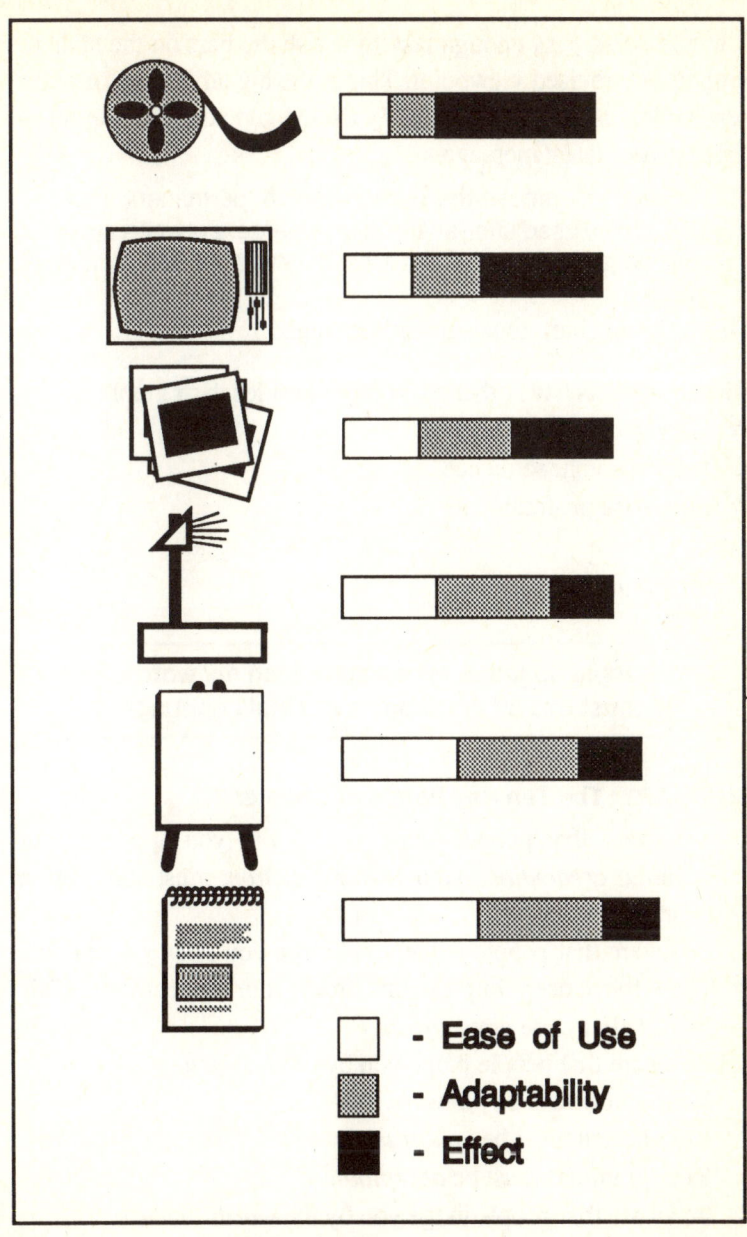

Visual Aids Comparison Chart

It would be an easy enough task to revise the bars on the slide to support any revised viewpoint. This is the big advantage of overhead slides. They may be so easily altered and adapted in order to support your latest message.

(Alcohol will remove the marks of even 'permanent' markers. I have used after-shave in an emergency, when away from base in an hotel. But I have never yet had to use whisky.)

The desk flip chart, too, is quickly changed.

Visual supports have other advantages besides their graphics.
☆ They give you confidence
☆ They cue your sequence
☆ They look professional

★ Realization

**People do judge me on more than my words.
I must use all the aspects of Total Language.**

SUMMARY: The Ten Key Points of Chapter 7.

1. Be aware that people judge you *before* you appear. Your acquired *credentials*, your own *reputation*, must stand up to their inquisition.

2. Be aware that people judge you before you *open your mouth*. They form deep impressions from your *appearance*. This should always be *appropriate*.

3. Be aware that people judge you by the *way you speak*.
   Your voice must be *pleasing*.
   Your accent must be *unobtrusive*.
   Your grammar must be *acceptable*.

4. Be aware that people judge you by the *words you use*.
   Use a *wide* vocabulary

But not *too* wide

Avoid 'low social' indicators

5. To acquire the *rhythm* of good speech listen to good speakers.

6. When you listen:

   Consider what you know of the speaker

   Examine the appearance of the speaker

   Note the way the speaker speaks.

   But do not miss the message!

7. Body Language—Outwards.

   Think positive and you will signal positive.

8. Body Language—Inwards.

   Know the common signs which can *support* your perceptions.

9. Use Visual Support that is *visible*.

10. Use Visual Support that *supports*.

EXERCISES

1. As a member of an audience, answer the following questions. Write your answers down. This commits you to think about your decisions, and you avoid snap judgements.

   (i) What do I know of this speaker?

   (ii) What can I tell from the speaker's appearance?

   (iii) What impression do I gain from the voice?

   (iv) Any jarring accent?

   (v) Any glaring errors of grammar?

   (vi) Any 'social' indicators?

   (vii) Words well or poorly used? (Note examples)

   This is a good exercise to help you to define your total impression of the speaker.

   Your notes should be a great help to the speaker, too. If you have the nerve to show them. And if the speaker has the good grace to accept them.

   If at all possible, try the above as a group training session. Everybody takes a turn to speak.

Everybody writes notes.

From the discussions generated by the observations the true learning really starts!

2. Your own 'Language Check'.

Many people like to 'put a figure' to things, so here is a way to score the effect of your speaking. The figures are loaded towards the more important elements. If you find it difficult to answer objectively, ask the opinion of others.

(i) *Your Voice*

Is it:	*Score*
Exciting and Effective?	35
Lively and above average?	25
With some life?	20
Monotonous and dreary?	5

(ii) *Your Accent*

Is it:	
Standard and not obtrusive?	15
Will pass (but you are conscious of it)?	10
Liable to drift down?	5
Really rough?	0

(iii) *Your Grammar*

Is it:	
Impeccable?	20
With occasional slips?	15
Good enough?	10
Obviously poor?	5

(iv) *Your Use of Words*

Wide-ranging vocabulary?	30
Good selection?	25

| Just manage? | 15 |
| Narrow range? | 5 |

Add up the total to give you a percentage and mark this on your calendar for three months ahead. On that date repeat the test.

If you have been working hard on the problem areas in the meantime, you will be able to measure an improvement. Which will be not only to your score, but to your everyday speech.

To help you to improve your speech on the aspects listed, and in other ways too, here is a '10 Easy Ways . . .' checklist.

Despite the good reputation you may have, and the fine way you may look, the 'Way you Speak' will remain the most important component of your Total Language.

Appendix:
10 Easy Ways to make Your Speaking More Better

1. Grammar. Watch it! Little errors show up (as above). (Listen to good speakers—in person & on radio. Read.)

2. Don't let your accent 'drift down'. (It is so easy to parrot-copy the bad habits of others.)

3. *Understand* the meanings of more words. (And use them.)

4. Don't repeat overworked and meaningless adjectives. (There are better bloody ways of bloody saying what you bloody mean.)

5. Make your words come alive. (Bring real live people into your examples.)

6. Wear a smile on your face. (Friendliness always helps.) Be sincere. (It shows if you aren't.)

7. Don't race when you speak. (There's no Grand Prix for the most words a minute.)

8. *Pause* after each idea, before going on. (So that your audience can absorb, and to allow you to prepare your next point.)

9. Don't be timid. Go for more *Life* in your voice. (Up and down, slow and fast, loud and soft—practice with a tape recorder.)

10. Don't hold back. Be *enthusiastic* and this will show. (Enthusiasm is infectious!)

Practise . . . Practise . . . Practise . . .

You have now been through seven chapters out of ten. (I hope that you have not been skipping about. This is a structured course.)

From your study, application, and practice of the principles set out, you should already have noticed an improvement in your communication skills, in your *day to day life*.

You should already show some PROFIT from your more EFFECTIVE COMMUNICATION.

- *From Chapter 1.*
  You should be planning and producing change to your advantage.

- *From Chapter 2.*
  You should be speaking confidently and clearly.

- *From Chapter 3.*
  You should be preparing well-organised and effective proposals.

- *From Chapter 4.*
  You should be gaining from your disciplined listening.

- *From Chapter 5.*
  You should be finding it easy to persuade people to agree.

- *From Chapter 6.*
  You should be winning most arguments.

- *From Chapter 7.*
  You should be giving full support to your spoken message.

In the next three chapters we will discuss:
— How to work well with people in discussion groups and committee meetings, and at interviews.
— How to write as well as you have learned to speak.
— How to add the final skills which will make you into a fully Effective Communicator.

8

Gain from meetings and interviews

Listen! Let me tell you why I think you must study this chapter.

What an awful opening! So abrasive. Almost as if I wanted to upset you, to make you bristle, to make you cross.

Let us analyse just why that opening is so bad.

Listen!	(You are jolted by this sharp command.)
Let me tell you	(You react: 'Why should I be ordered about?')
why I think	('I can think for myself, thank you.')
you must study this chapter.	('Dictatorship')

So would I gain your interest and co-operation?
Never.
Yet this example is no worse than many of the opening words which assail our ears every day. And it is better than most . . .

'I've decided how you must present your figures.'
'Listen! Here is your next move.'
'Don't do it like *that*!'

The common factor, as you can see, is 'Ordering people about'. This does have to be done. You do have to tell people what to do. But to do this successfully, so that they will take orders happily, you should follow three of the basic rules which we have already set.

1. *Headline* your subject.
2. Offer a *Benefit*.
3. *Suggest* the change.

■ **This chapter is about working with people.**
■ **You will learn how to gain their goodwill.**
■ **So you should study it all carefully.**

   Which is another way with the same opening.
   And isn't it so much better?

As you are not a hermit living in a cave, you will find yourself meeting up with people every day. Groups of people. Family, friends, colleagues, strangers . . . Groups of people who Live, Love, Work, and Play.

The people in these groups communicate. They talk, they listen. As a result of their communication, ideas are brought forth, decisions are made, actions are taken.

Change takes place.

In any group in which you might find yourself, you can play the dummy. Dummies say nothing. Dummies listen to nothing. If you choose to play the dummy, the group will move forward without you. Changes will continue to take place. But you will have had no part in them.

To *participate* in all that is going on, to be fully alive, you must *contribute* to every group you may find yourself to be in. You must speak up. You must listen. You must use your new skills of argument and of persuasion. The better you participate, the better off you will be. The more you will profit.

The groups which we will consider are:

Social Conversations
Discussion Groups
Committees

Followed by the Art of the Successful Interview.

But first, some discussion on that other very important art.

⇨ The Art of Understanding people.

At Cross Purposes

You will have had the feeling, 'I cannot get on with this person. There is something about them that sets me on edge.'

Which does happen. We do meet jarring people. The situation has been described as 'vibrating in opposing planes'. Your vibes are sideways, theirs are up and down. So you never can relate.

In a social situation you can turn and walk away. But in business —well, the repellant one might be Big News. So you will have to make the best of it. You will have to try to talk.

I have a friend who never has this problem. She is able to talk freely to the most awkward-seeming of people. 'How do you do it?' I asked.

'I keep free of all prejudice. And then I can understand them. It's as easy as that.'

This is full understanding, in the widest sense. And to reach this happy state we have to realise that other people are *different* from ourselves. Not blacker, or whiter, or better, or worse. Only different. With their own interests, their own point of view.

You have to see things *their* way. You have to tune to *their* vibrations. So that the barrier can fall away.

Thing-People and People-People

People divide into two groups:

> Those interested in *Things*.
> Those interested in *People*.

I will describe the extremes, but few of us are extremes. Most of us are somewhere in between.

Although some do lean towards things

While others lean towards people

The archtype interested in **THINGS**

> Collects. Hoards. Seldom throws anything away.
> Does not like to move house.

An extreme true case:

> I was at a newly rebuilt railway terminus in London, waiting for the night train to Scotland. It was a Sunday evening. I had expected the restaurant to be open. But it wasn't. So, instead of a long leisurely dinner to take up the time, I had had to be content with a quick snack. Which now left me with a two hour wait. I sat on my suitcase. Most uncomfortable. But there were no seats. A strange omission.
>
> Some days later, curious about this lack of seating, I phoned British Rail, and I found out why. 'It's the Station Manager, sir. He doesn't want people sitting around in the new concourse. He thinks that people would make the place look untidy.'

The archtype interested in **PEOPLE**

> Possessions have little meaning.
> Cars are for moving from A to B.

The extreme case:

> Would be very happy singing along with all the others in a choir.

The very extreme case:

> Would only sing solo.

Permanent-People and Transient-People

People divide into two groups:

> Those who like *Permanence*.
> Those who like *Transience*.

I will describe the extremes, but few of us are extremes.
Most of us are somewhere in between.

> Although some lean towards permanence
> While others lean towards transience

The archtype interested in **PERMANENCE**

> Works to put things together.
> Wants them to stay in place for ever.

An extreme true case:

> He laboured away at his front lawn. He spread fertilizer, he rolled, he tended, he weeded. His lawn was perfect, for a while. Then he had to start all over again.
> So he had his front garden concreted over. He laid plastic grass. Which would remain smooth and green for ever.

The archtype interested in **TRANSIENCE**

> Lives for today.
> Has no interest in the past, no interest in the future.
> Good examples are those on the stage.
> To them all that matters is this play, this performance, and the applause that is ringing in their ears.

Know your Audience, and Know Yourself

I am not asking you to become an instant psychoanalyst. But I am asking you to consider the dominant traits in those to whom you speak, and in yourself, so that you may understand the differences, know the polarities, and be able to work with all you meet.

You will not be able to instantly analyse the members of a 'new' audience, who are all unknown to you. But most of the

people you meet socially and in business are not total strangers.
— Your clients or customers
— Your colleagues
— The fellow-members of a Board or Committee

All of these you can learn to know well.

People/Things and Permanence/Transience are but two of the polarising influences that can set people apart. And which can cause them to think, talk, and behave as individuals. They are different from one another. And they are different from you.

Other opposing measures are:

Fast to react/Slow to react
Introverted/Extroverted
Emotional/Tranquil
And there are many more . . .

PROFIT FROM KNOWING PEOPLE BETTER

It is sensitivity to the characteristics of the other person that enables some husbands and wives to know and understand one another so well after only a few months of marriage.

While other couples remain strangers to each other forever . . .

You must know and understand the other person if you are to live with them happily.

Or work with them effectively.

And, know a group one by one as individuals, and that group is no longer made up of strangers.

Social Conversations

Earlier in the book we noted that those who shine in social conversation are also good in business discussion. This versatility is no coincidence. This same need for a feeling for others, the same need for understanding, applies to both skills.

Egotists, who want to talk all the time, and about themselves, do not make good conversationalists. Nor are they particularly good in business discussions.

They may force the issue. 'Because I am the boss, see!' But that is not good management.

'Why doesn't anybody ever co-operate?' That is the astonished plea of the unfeeling boss-person.

Many people live out on the borders of conversations, not participating, because they are shy. So they do not gain the practice, the self-assurance, the ability to speak up, that they need in order to take part fully in the discussions at their place of work.

Here are a few quick tips for overcoming shyness, in the context of conversations. (Those lucky ones who are not shy may skip this section.)

1. *No, they won't laugh*

   People do not wait eagerly, hoping that you will say something stupid. People are generally kind.

2. *You must talk to be noticed*
   This is another point which we have mentioned before. Stay silent and you will be ignored. Speak up and people will turn in your direction.

3. *How to break into a conversation*
   A seemingly-impossible hurdle for the shy. Somebody else is always talking. How do I get a turn?
   — Move in on a pause.
     'See what I mean? . . .' And they pause.
     Now! In you go.
   — Derail the train of thought.
     No pauses? Interrupt with a new subject. Startling if possible.
     'I hear that we are to have new neighbours.'

4. *Conversation among complete strangers*
   Ask an opinion. Few can resist turning to you with a reply. They will then wait for your reaction.

Once you realise how easy it is to take part in a conversation with the strangest of strangers, or with the most prepossessing of pragmatists, you will find yourself quite capable of holding your own in the toughest of business meetings.

Discussion Groups

— The purpose of a discussion is for people to be able to talk together in order to share their thoughts.
— A discussion can be between two people, but usually involves a group.
— For a formal discussion the group will be brought together by arrangement. For an informal discussion they gather spontaneously.
— The discussion is normally concerned with a single topic.
— The usual purpose of a discussion is to solve a specific problem.

Almost automatically, the discussion will follow a set sequence:

1. The problem is stated.
2. Ideas are gathered.
3. There is give and take. (Compromise)
4. A solution is agreed upon. (Consensus)
5. Responsibility for action is set.

Crisis in a Toothpaste Factory

In which you will note the important point played by the leader of the group in guiding and controlling the discussion.

> **General Manager:** 'I've called you together today to discuss the low profits last month.'

Clearly states the problem. Good.

> **Financial Manager:** 'Profits were down because sales were down. It's as simple as that.'
> **Sales Manager:** 'Sales were down because of that gritty batch that went out, that's why.'

> **Works Manager:** 'Every batch has been within spec. Why blame me?'

And so it goes on. Classic passing of the buck. But we have a wise General Manager who knows that low profits are a symptom, not the problem. This is very often the case. The true underlying problem has to be searched out. So he turns to the Product Manager . . .

> **General Manager:** 'You are very quiet, Jim. What do you think?'

> **Product Manager:** 'Our "Pearlglo" has lost its impact, as I've been telling people all year.'

> **General Manager:** 'Well you haven't been telling the right people. You have said nothing to me. Tell us about it now.'

The Product Manager reminds them that a toothpaste has a life cycle. It is launched with a boost of promotion, customer awareness is gained and then maintained with advertising, but eventually all novelty has gone and sales decline. He finishes off with:

> Product Manager: 'There are new products competing against us with new features. "Pearlglo" has had its day. No financial juggling, no quality campaigns, no extra advertising can save it now. As I've been saying all year.'

The negative pessimist. There is one at every meeting.

> General Manager: Yes, yes. So we are now aware of the real problem. We have an obsolete product. Do we all agree?'

With their nods of assent he proceeds.

> 'Right! Let's hear your ideas. How can we pep up our ailing brand?'

This is the 'Brainstorming' session. The call for contributions.

Rules for a successful Brainstorm:

☆ The more ideas the better

☆ They must be written up (board, flipchart, overhead projector) for all to see

☆ Way out ideas welcomed

☆ Build one idea upon another

☆ Stop when ideas fall off

Then identify and discuss the possibles.

> 'What we need is a new flavour.'
> 'I came across a whisky flavoured toothpaste over in the States.'
> 'How about chocolate chip?'

And so on and so on . . .

From this particular brainstorm comes the decision to investigate an effervescent toothpaste. Although not a flavour, it was the discussion on flavours that sparked the idea.

The General Manager now calls a halt to the session. He appoints the Technical Manager to report back at the next meeting on the feasibility and cost of producing a fizzy toothpaste.

> Most meetings go on for too long. Several short meetings are usually more effective. Short meetings stay alive. And there can be progress outside of, and between, them.

At the follow-up meeting next day:

> Technical Manager: 'We have made good progress. Everybody is very keen. We have produced samples that fizz.'
> 'And which stay fizzy, even after the tube has been opened?'
> 'Yes.'
> 'This could well be the unique selling point we need.'
> 'The more conservative customers might not accept . . .'
> 'How soon can we do this?'
> 'Has anybody checked the costs?'
> 'How about a punchy new name?'

All of these varied points are important. They all need to be discussed. And they are discussed.

Finally:

> General Manager: 'We are all agreed then? The idea is desirable and it is feasible. So fizzy toothpaste it is!'

> Supplies Manager (he has not spoken before; he is the type who stays silent until the very end, then throws a spanner wrapped in a wet blanket into the works, as he does now): 'We have over six months' stock of "Pearlglo" in factory stores. That is worth a lot of money. What does anybody propose to do with all this stock?'

Occasionally such people do produce a genuine objection. But usually not.

> Sales Manager: 'We can phase the launch into various areas, to use up all old stock.'

Which is the answer to that one. Some adjustment, some compromise, is usually necessary.

Very finally:

> General Manager: 'Right then! We are agreed. Thank you all for your contributions. Next we must get on to discuss responsibilities and to set target dates.'

This is important. So many meetings end and fade away once the problem has been solved. Everybody pats themselves upon the back and then they all go off for lunch.

It is *essential* that responsibilities be set.

- Somebody must be appointed to carry out each part of the required change.

- Dates for the completion of each stage need to be set.

Otherwise nothing very much will happen . . .

Before any Meeting

You will have been told the subject to be discussed. You will probably already know something of the possible problems. So study up on their implications.

There is no need to appear at the gathering knowing less than you should.

At any Meeting

Do not:

— Project yourself instead of your contribution.

  'Well with all my experience I think . . .'

— Introduce conflict on a personal basis.

  'It's all very well for *you* to talk . . .'

— Be against it all on principle.

  'We tried that once and it didn't work . . .'

But do:

- Speak up on what you think.

- Listen to what others think.

- Go along with majority decisions.

After the Meeting

A dilemma.

You attended the 'toothpaste' meeting. You agreed with all that was decided. You accepted the name for the new product. 'Fizzo'.

Now, some time later, you suddenly wake in the night. Your subconscious has come up with a perfect name, 'Sparkles'.

So what should you do?

Tell somebody?

Keep quiet?

I suggest that you should phone the General Manager, first thing at the office next morning. Mention this new name. Emphasise that it came to you suddenly *after* the meeting. (If he should suspect that you thought of the perfect name *at* the meeting, but were too shy to speak up, then he will kill you.)

It is his factory, his meeting, his problem. So let him decide. As he is a good General Manager he will most probably first consult with the Advertising Agency (who are the experts on names). If they like this new suggestion, then he must ask the views of all who were at the meeting.

Confidential note from GM: New name.
The name 'Sparkles' has now been suggested for our new brand as an alternative to 'Fizzo'. Should you have any definite objection then please phone me urgently.

From the reaction to this he will be able to make a clear decision.

Harmony

To be a useful member of a discussion group you must understand all the other members.

They are people like yourself.

So be open, frank, and friendly. And they will be open, frank, and friendly back.

■ **People, working together in harmony,
  make wise decisions.**

■ **Harmonious people get things done.**

PROFIT FROM WORKING WITH PEOPLE

COMMITTEES!!

The very word causes most of us to react.

'What an outlet for hot air!'

'What an utter waste of time!'

'A Committee is a meeting together of a group of people who singly can do nothing, and who collectively decide that nothing can be done.'

All true. Committees can be a pain.

If you work and live alone.
If you belong to no Clubs, Societies, or Associations.
If you show no concern for anybody than yourself.

Then you may be able to avoid having to 'serve on a committee'.

There are alternatives to Committees:

Autocratic Rule

If nobody is prepared to discuss matters in committee and come to a joint decision, then somebody in power will be only too happy to make all the decisions, and that's that.

Tribal Elders

Decisions are made for the majority by a minority who are in senior positions.

This does not always work. Not all Senior Councillors, not all members of Boards of Directors, have attained wisdom. Some have merely grown old.

Round and Round and Round

It used to be the custom among some Central African tribes for the men of the village to gather to sit around in a large circle, all being equal in status.

One would then shout out his proposal, which would be repeated by all around the circle in turn. They would use the exact same words if in agreement, they would change them to suit their own ideas if not.

Round and round the proposal would go, until eventually all had spoken the exact same words for one complete circuit.

Which was *a* way to reach true consensus, but it did take time. Often until the sun went down . . . Longer than many a committee meeting . . .

And this is saying something.

Back to the Committee

> 'Much of the time of a committee is taken up in deciding upon the date for the next meeting.'

True enough. Committees are inefficient. They do waste time. But until a better alternative is discovered we seem to be stuck with them.

The Committee System does allow for full discussion of an issue, that can be said for it. And any full discussion, people being people, and all wanting their fair say, is bound to drag on . . .

Getting Things Done

Now what is the real basic purpose of a committee?
Any committee? I would say:

■ TO BRING ABOUT CHANGE

1. By heeding the views of the majority towards the promotion of needed change.
2. By making sure that such change *does take place*.

It is as simple as that.

How smoothly the process goes through, does depend very much upon the efficiency of whoever is in the chair.

When You are in the Chair!

As the Chairperson in charge of a committee you have three definite and important duties.

1. You have to be a *Pilot*.
2. You have to be a *Referee*.
3. You have to be an *Activator*.

As **PILOT**

Before your meeting:

— Plan, prepare, and circulate the agenda.

At your meeting:
— Guide progress through the agenda, one point at a time.
— If nobody is taking minutes or notes then you must.

As **REFEREE**

— Assure justice and courtesy for all.
— The majority rules, the minority has a right to be heard.
☆ *Control* your meeting.
☆ *Insist* that everything said is said 'through the chair'.
☆ *Stamp out* any private discussions. One meeting at a time!
On any outbreak of noise or chatter, *Call to Order* immediately.
(Rap on table with gavel, glass, or fist.)
☆ *Order* any unruly member to leave meeting.

As an **ACTIVATOR**

As we noted in the toothpaste factory, no decision to change is of
any use at all until the change decided upon has actually taken
place.

It is a part of your task, when in the Chair, to activate all decisions
made.

This means:
— Decide, with agreement:
☆ *Who* is to make the change
  Possibly also '*How*'
  And certainly '*By When*'
☆ *Confirm* all of this to the 'Who', preferably in writing.
☆ *Keep a Check* on progress until all is complete.
Your responsibility does not end until all resolutions to change,
made under your command, have been carried out.

It is all common-sense really.

Parliamentary Procedure

All common-sense departs from Committee Room or Board Room when 'Parliamentary Procedure' is insisted upon.

Much of this procedure is completely nonsensical, outside of a parliament, and it is not always so marvellous inside of a parliament either.

You will still find people pushing 'the proper way to do things' into your meetings. They do this for two main reasons—to show themselves up as so clever, and to try to show you up as ignorant.

When such a person 'Arises on a point of privilege' your best response is, 'So what are you on about now? Please explain.'

Further to the use of more common-sense in all meetings—everywhere—I have two more axes to grind. This could raise a shower of sparks, especially my views on Seconding, but there we are.

Motions

☆ A motion must *propose some change*.
'I would like to propose that the balance sheet has been very clearly set out this year.'
Chair: 'Thank you. Would you like to make that a vote of thanks to our Accountant?'
Which is a change for the Accountant. Nobody has every thanked him for anything before.

☆ The motion must be *short and clear*.
If the intent is not clear then you, in the Chair, have the responsibility to make it so. You have to re-phrase the words, working with the proposer's permission, until all is clear.

Everybody knows that the amendment must be voted upon before the motion, but not everybody is sure why.

Motion: That coffee be served at morning break instead of tea.

Amendment: That tea be available for those who may want it.

Tea-drinkers would not be able to decide which way to vote on this motion, until the matter of availability of tea has been decided.

'Seconding'

Every meeting has its professional seconders. You will know them. At the mention of the word 'second' their hands fly up in a reflex movement. Perhaps it is to get their names in the minutes?

There can also be a nut at every meeting, who will raise nutty motions. At the Cricket Club AGM a nut proposes, 'I know. Let's bowl from both ends at once, for a brighter game.'

The purpose of asking for a seconder is to show that nut is on nut's own with nut's nutty suggestion. Nobody will second—in theory. But of course somebody will. Either by reflex, or because it is quite possible to have more than one nut at a meeting.

Common-sense solution:

Rather call for support—
'Do I have the support of the meeting for this rather unusual proposal to be discussed?'
There will be little support, if any.
So, 'Sorry. You are on your own.'

With nominations, too, it makes good sense to call for 'Some facts in favour of your candidate' from both nominator and supporter, who takes the place of a seconder.

This is far more informative to everybody, and more useful, than the usual singing out of names.

Streamline the Procedures

Plan to improve the efficient running of any committee on which you serve. It is your own time you will save.

■ **Use your common-sense.**
■ **Do not be put off with, 'But we have always done things this way.'**

And one final word for anybody involved in any committee:

Co-operate! You are part of a team.

Interviews

Many people, on hearing the word 'interview', immediately think of a job interview. But there are many more applications than that . . .

An interview moves information from one person to another through the asking and answering of questions.

- The person being interviewed is the key person.

- It is the *answering* of the questions that transfers the information.

Although good questioning undoubtably does help. The better the questioning, the better the replies.

Skilled questioning is used:

- As in a Court of Law (to build up a case)

- To help the nervous (and draw out the facts)

- To control the interview (and keep it to subject)

The questions and answers can alternate.

Husband and wife, trying to balance their budget:
He: 'Could we eat less meat, do you think?'
She: 'That's a possibility . . . And could you take sandwiches for lunch?'

The questions can be one-to-many.

You, as detective: 'Who left the lights on all night?'

The questions can be many-to-one.

The selection panel, interviewing the quivering candidate.

When you are *Asking the Questions*.

To be effective as a questioner (which means obtaining useful answers) you have to do some advance thinking.

— What *results* do I want? (Not answers . . . if you knew the answers you would not need to interview.)

— What am I looking for? Information? Opinion? Solution? Reason?

Or perhaps a combination of all four?

— What sort of person will I be interviewing? (Background? Nervous or confident? Open or reticent?) If you do not know this sort of information in advance, then you will have to establish it with your first few questions.

You will need to prepare some series of key questions, with some structure to them, but you will also need to retain flexibility. Many of your most useful questions will be suggested by the answers to others as you go along. The ticking off of questions down a fixed list is the mark of the amateur.

Who broke the Photostat Machine?

A useful basic structure in action.

1. 'Good morning Janet, and how are you today?'
   (To put her at her ease)

2. 'Can you advise us about the machine?'
   (We need your help)

3. 'Is it the machine at fault, do you think? Or the people who work it?'
   (Offer her a choice)

4. 'So you say that too many people fiddle with the settings?'
   (Confirm her statement)

5. 'Any other comments?'
   (Look for any other alternatives)

6. 'So you say that one person should be put in charge?'
   (Confirm her opinion)

When you are Answering the Questions

Ask yourself in advance:
— What is the purpose of this interview?
  (So that you will understand the intention of the questioner.)
— What can I expect to gain?
  (So that you will be motivated by the potential benefits to yourself.)

Prepare:
— Think ahead about your answers to likely questions.
— At the interview, do your best to help.
  By giving your answers clearly and concisely.
  By asking your own questions if you do not understand.

The Job Interview

How not to do it. You may not believe this, but here are some actual replies which I jotted down in the course of a single session of interviewing applicants. It was a fairly high-grade position on offer, too.

'Why are you asking me all this?'

(No idea of purpose)

'I haven't thought about the type of job I want. Actually.'

(No planning)

'I would have brought some of my certificates, if I had only thought . . .'

(No preparation)

'Well, I did have an uncle in Somerset West who used to do this sort of work. I think.'

(Way off course)

'No, don't stop me. I want to tell you something.'

(Lacking in co-operation)

So, have you learned anything? Do you think you are bright enough to be able to handle an interview?

This remark makes you *bristle*. And quite rightfully too.

A poorly worded question can upset the person being questioned.
— This is the questioner's fault.

A person with too sensitive an attitude can be upset by a quite normal question.
'You've got a nerve! Asking my age!'
— This is the questionee's fault.

Failure of understanding, on either side, can spoil an interview.
Friendly co-operation is the name of the game.

Briefing and Debriefing

You will often need to brief somebody, or a group, on some change which you intend to be brought about.

When Briefing:
1. Suggest that notes be taken
2. Explain the requirements clearly
3. Ask: 'Any questions?'
4. Repeat the requirements
5. Obtain assurance of understanding.

Later, after the change has taken place, the task completed, there will need to be a report back.

The Debriefing:
1. Ask, 'How did it go?'
   Anything not completed?
   Any alterations necessary?
   Any snags to report?
   Anything else to mention?

2. Thank all who took part.

It is likely that you will *be* briefed, on occasion.
When being briefed:
1. Be ready to take notes
2. 'Think as you listen' (What is this going to entail?)
3. Look through any written information handed out
4. Ask if you are not sure.

And when being debriefed:
1. Have notes ready
2. Explain how it went
3. Detail any difficulties
4. Assure 'Required Change Complete'.

Such short simple rules! But if everybody did just this, then Industry and Commerce would glide on greased wheels.

 Realization!

In order to work with people I need to understand people.

SUMMARY: The Ten Key Points of Chapter 8

You and Them

1. *Consider* your opening remarks and the effect upon other people.
2. *Consider* that all other people are different to yourself.

Conversations

3. You must *talk* to be *noticed*.
4. *Claim* your share of the conversation.

Discussions

5. Should *air* views, *resolve* conflicts, *accept* compromise, *agree* on action.
6. To make a discussion work for you, *prepare* and *participate*.

Committees

7. In the Chair, you need to *Pilot, Referee,* and *Activate.*
8. The *efficiency* of any committee can be improved by using common-sense.

Interviews

9. To gain information ask the *right questions.* To give information give the *right replies.*

Briefing/Debriefing

10. Before: *Explain* exactly what you want. After: *Ask about* any deviations from plan.

EXERCISES

1. For the slightly shy
   For a week, make a point of opening a conversation with at least one total stranger, every day.
   Mark your calendar for each 'Conversational Conquest'.
   (These are conquests for you, over your shyness. You do not need to open up and win arguments!)
2. For everybody
   Gather a group of friends. Make a game of classifying one another. As:
   Thing People/People People
   Permanent People/Transient People
   Fast to react/Slow to react
   Introverted/Extroverted

Emotional/Tranquil

And by at least one other classification of your own devising.

3. Select three of your colleagues or friends. Using the same classifications, but without consultation, write down how you feel they compare to yourself.

4. Determine that you will work in harmony and with common-sense in any discussion group or committee in which you might find yourself.

9

Write letters and reports that work

It is a wet Saturday afternoon. Young Kathy is bored. She has tried to phone all of her best friends, but none of them is at home. She has ruffled through her stack of discs—they are all so *old*, and there is nothing to read, either. She goes and turns on the telly . . . Horse racing! b-o-r-i-n-g . . . So now here she lies on her tummy on her bed and she thinks, 'Why does life have to be so utterly dull?'

Later, at table, her Mother asks, 'Well, I hope you found a chance to write your thank-you letter to your Uncle.'

'Never had the time.'

Writing a letter is such an *effort*.

'I'll phone him sometime,' Kathy says.

Her Dad looks up. 'A phone call is not the same.'

And of course it isn't. And Kathy knows it isn't. She knows that her Uncle expects a letter, that he will *appreciate* a letter, be so pleased that she has taken the trouble. By sending him a letter she will be making sure of a nice cheque next year for her birthday, too.

'I'll write in the morning,' she says, 'Instead of going to church.'

Forcing oneself to write a letter, or in fact to force oneself down to writing anything, is hard work, there is no doubt about it. We all suffer so easily from writer's block. But writing is a task that so often has to be done.

In this chapter we will discuss the writing of letters, both social and business, which you will have to do, the writing of reports, which you will probably have to do, and the writing of short memos, which you are unlikely to be using enough, if at all.

All of which skills will add to your total command of 'Effective Communication'. Through the control of the written word you will be able to set your own ideas firmly into other people's minds. Profitably.

We will start with personal letters.

PROFIT FROM YOUR CLEAR WRITING

Why personal letters? In a book intended mainly for the business person?

☆ Once you can write a good personal letter you can *communicate in writing*. Your thoughts, your words, your emotions.

☆ Once you can communicate in writing you can soon learn to write *anything*. Business correspondence, reports, technical notes, instruction leaflets . . . Anything. Quite easily.

A Table of Difficulty

— A letter to a good friend, written a few days into your first visit overseas.
— A letter to a family member, to complain of a broken promise.
— A letter to an elderly relative, as a thank-you for a present.
— A letter to the headmaster (mistress) of your old school, on the occasion of its centenary.
— A letter to the wife of a colleague, after his sudden death from a heart attack.

I am sure that you will agree that this table is set out in order of difficulty. To write of exciting news to a good friend is so easy, while what to write after a bereavement can be a very great problem indeed. There are some interesting points to note:

Looking at the recipients of the letters, the table progresses by *how well each is known to you.* The wife of your colleague *was* a close friend. Now suddenly, as a widow, she has become distant. This awful thing has come between you. You can no longer relate.

This should not happen, of course. She needs your friendship now more than ever. She has not changed. Your attitude has.

Think of her as a lonely person, needing confirmation of your friendship, know her better, and this becomes not so difficult a letter to write after all.

It is easy to write to people you *know.*

Just as it is easy to speak to people you know.

• You have learned to *think about and understand* those you talk to.

• In the same way you need to *think about and understand* those you write to.

Everybody is basically a person not that much different from yourself.

Looking again at this same series of letters, note that there will be less and less enthusiasm for writing them as they become more difficult.

(And it is revealing to note the general preference towards writing letters of complaint, rather than towards writing letters of praise!)

Build up your enthusiasm! In difficult cases think more of the pleasures of the letter being read, rather than of your struggle to write it.

☆ *Be enthusiastic* and it is easy to talk well.

☆ *Be enthusiastic* and it is easy to write well.

Your enthusiasm comes from:

• Wanting to tell the other person your news

• Wanting to share your thoughts

• Wanting them to feel the same as you

■ **Open up! A personal letter must be *personal*.**
■ **This is the simple secret.**

More Hints:

Some people do experience a genuine 'block'. They can chatter away very successfully, but with pen in hand their minds go quite numb. 'What can I say?' This 'say' is the clue. Letter writing should be approached as being a conversation—a one-way conversation it is true—rather than an effort of *writing down* lofty and significant thoughts which *will not come*.

What would you talk about to this particular person, face to face? Yourself? Something interesting that has happened to you? Something you have done today?

To somebody who cares about you, a simple account of your day can be most interesting. Even the simple description of 'What the dog did' can bring happiness to a homesick member of the family, far away . . .

- But people should not write only of themselves. (Which are the bits you like best in the letters *you* get? The bits about you, not so?)

- Mousy little introverts can write the most wonderful letters. They open their hearts, they tell their innermost feelings, they come *alive* in their written words.
  Why is this? How are they able to project themselves so well? I think it is a transfer or responsibility, along the same lines as when a glove puppet is given to a shy child. The puppet becomes most amazingly chatty. (It is not *me* talking, it is the dolly.) And so with the shy letter writer. (This is not *me*, writing these words. My hand is working away, outside of myself.) You may not be a mousy little introvert, but there is nothing to stop you writing with the same full freedom. Let your inner feelings tell you what to say, let your uninhibited writing hand move free.

- Good social letter writing is becoming a lost art. And a telephone call is not the same.

A Different Medium

So there are certain similarities between speaking and writing. And there are certain differences too. Similarities first.

- Both the spoken and the written word can be used to bring about change. (In the Level of Knowledge of others, in the Attitude of others, and in their Behaviour and Course of Action. Remember?
- The *purpose* may remain the same.
- But the *medium* changes.

☆ The written word is not the same as the spoken word written down.

☆ The spoken word is not the same as the written word read out aloud.

There are important differences in the medium.

The Four Main Differences

1. One-Way Communication:

    'You write so well on your subject,' I said, 'Will you come to give us a lecture?'

    'I never lecture. I can't take all those staring eyes.'

    For those not prepared to conquer their fear of speaking from a platform, or even to a small group, the alternative of writing down their message, all alone with their thoughts, is a happy refuge. But there is a penalty. Without the feedback of a live audience there is no personal contact. Writers can so easily become isolated, quite out of touch with the human reaction essential to their work.

    (We noted this lack of two-way communication when we discussed reading. The reader can scribble 'Nonsense!' in a margin. Which the writer seldom sees.)

2. Opportunity to Refine:

    Because the writer can proceed at a leisurely pace, taking care and trouble to choose every word and to revise each sentence, the written word can be more polished. But it is *expected* to be more polished. The written word is *expected* to be right. Slovenly word usage which we easily get away with when speaking, shows up against us on the written—and even more on the printed—page. That is another characteristic of the written word. It can be so permanent.

3. Permanence:

    Your written words can linger, long after you have forgotten them . . .

— A business letter, emerging from an ancient file, can prove awkward.

— A love letter, surfacing from some hidden place, can prove embarrassing.

You have to be so much more careful of what you write than of what you say.

> **Spoken words waft away and are forgotten.**
> **Written words stay there.**

4. Unknown Recipients:

    You know your listeners. You can see them. There they are in front of you.

    But who will read what you sit down to write? Readers are a great unknown, spread out in time and in space.

    This is a great problem for the writers of mail-order missives.

    — They try so hard to appear personal.

    'This is the holiday *you* have dreamed of . . .'

    — They try so hard for immediacy.

    'Take advantage of this *new* offer . . .'

    But even though their computers sprinkle our names so generously, for all the 'Now!' 'Today!' and 'You alone!', we are not fooled. This is a circular letter, one of thousands, junk mail. 98% of us throw such letters away.

A wide and unknown readership can also be a problem for you, sitting there late at night, writing the special report requested by your boss. You do not know who will eventually see it, up through the organisation as well as down, so you have to be so very careful. You think and consider, and feel that you should tone down your message, and it loses some of its punch.

Support the Spoken Word with the Written

Use spoken and written word together and they both gain. The short lifespan of the words you speak can be extended in longer lasting print. The impersonal one-wayness of the words you write can be enlivened by the warmth of speech.

Examples: Supporting speech.

1. Those who attend Press Conferences are given reference notes.
2. A firm of financial advisers follows up every interview, every important telephone call, with a letter. This confirms the matters discussed and details the actions to be taken. Explains the manager: 'A short letter is better than a long misunderstanding.'

Examples: Personalising your words.

1. I know of a top Salesman who, after he has sent in his Sales Report, phones his Sales Manager. He asks if there are any points to be discussed. This thoroughness is one of the reasons why he is a Top Salesman. The Sales Manager has to read this man's report first, too. Carefully. Ready for the call.
2. 'Dad, can we talk for a moment about how hard I try at school? Before you read my report . . .'

Business Letters

I noted the following advice in a book on 'How to Write Business Letters' and I do not agree.

If the letter you are answering is rude, be courteous.

If the letter you are answering is muddled, be straightforward.

If the letter you are answering is confused, be clear.

No 'ifs' about it!

All business letters should be courteous, and straightforward, and clear, at all times. Whether you are answering or initiating.

But many of them, unfortunately, are not. Many otherwise normal people become officious, and patronising, and pig-headed, as well as rude, muddled, and confused when writing a letter 'for the firm'. Especially if there becomes the slightest opportunity to show up the other firm as 'wrong'. Perhaps the authority of the letterhead excites them. So they pounce upon the slightest misunderstanding. They turn any exchange into a duel.

No wonder that clients and customers get upset! And you might have somebody like this working for you.

Know the results you want

When you have to start any correspondence, perhaps the first notice to an unsuspecting customer to advise that payments are way behind, forget the form letter, which is as cold water. Rather send a warm friendly note, explaining plainly what you want to happen, and why.

'Please settle this account or we will have to stop deliveries.' A little longer, of course, but to this effect.

Know what you Answer

In the normal way of things, most business correspondence is in reply to other correspondence, so first study the file. Be sure that you know the background up to now.

Next study this new letter, to be answered.
What does this letter ask? What is wanted?

Information?
Give it. Resist the temptation to over-elaborate.

Action?
If the action is possible, confirm that it will happen, and by when.
If it is not possible, explain why. Give reasons, not excuses.

Correction of your mistake?
If true, admit, apologise, and promise to correct.
If not true, explain the misunderstanding. Carefully.

Which all means that you need to *think*.

- About the letter

- About your reply

- About the fact that this is a *person* you are writing to, not unlike yourself. With needs, brains, and feelings.

Elementary? Well see what actually happens. Here are some comments on a rather poor letter written to me.

1. My name was incorrectly spelled.
   Inexcusable. Guaranteed to upset.

2. 'Here are the alternatives, and we have chosen for you . . .
   '*I* wanted to choose.

3. 'We trust that you can afford this.'
   This is rude.

4. A page and a half of technical detail, involved proofs, and general crowing. All to prove me wrong on one small point. I am neither unreasonable nor stupid. Few people are. Explain to me simply and I will understand.

5. 'May we look forward to your further esteemed custom?'
   No.

Know who you answer

Each person out there is much like yourself. Each has needs, brains, and feelings. And each is an individual. Consider this in each letter you write. For any letter to be successful the recipient must feel, 'This is for me alone.'

This is the one big fault with so many business letters. Their whole content, their whole tone, their whole arms-length attitude, signals 'This is a message from a firm to a firm' or 'From a firm to poor insignificant little you'. And it will be a rather dull message, at that.

All business letters, however dry their subject, can gain some human content by being person-to-person.

You may be writing on behalf of your firm to another firm, but set custom aside. For a live message it must be to somebody, addressed by name, clearly signed by name.

Besides, a 'Dear Sirs' letter can end up with anybody. Or with the right person, but two days late.

Here is an example of a customer (you) complaining to a Motor Dealer. That is, a person to a firm, the sort of complaint which seems so often to carry little weight.

First—phone. Make sure of the name of their Service Manager, and of his initials, too.

Ah, you say. Why not ask to speak to the man, then? Why write a letter?

— You can be sure that your complaint is written out exact and correct.

— A letter does not encourage quick off-the-cuff excuses.

— A letter goes on file.

Mr R G McMillen
Service Manager
A to B Motors

Dear Mr McMillen,

I am the customer who complained to you about grease left on the steering wheel of my car.

It has happened again.

Please instruct your mechanics not to wipe their greasy hands on steering wheels.
Or you will lose my custom.

Sincerely
. . .

Points to note:

1. *Headline* on what it is about ('I am the customer . . .')
   Update on 'level of knowledge' (It has happened again . . .')
   Action to be taken ('Please instruct . . .')
   Persuasion by the offering of avoidance of 'potential loss of benefit'. ('Or you will lose my custom.')

2. The 'Change of attitude to agree with me' is not stated but it is implied.

3. The temptation to be sarcastic should be avoided. ('You should provide a row of old steering wheels for them to wipe their hands on.')
   The temptation to be facetious should be avoided. ('Do they use steering wheels for towels at home?')
   Written sarcasm and facetiousness seldom accomplish any- thing. Come to that, spoken sarcasm and facetiousness are not all that successful either. Except for making enemies.

4. 'Dear' means 'Beloved'. This Service Manager is not beloved by you, and neither is the Receiver of Revenue, nor are many of the other people you have to write to in the course of business, for that matter. 'Dear . . .' is an accepted convention. I would not like to be the first to try to change it.

5. 'Sincerely' is becoming the accepted salutation for the ending of a business letter, with the use of 'Yours faithfully' dropping away.
   I went through a short season of ending off with 'Cordially Yours' in the accepted American manner, but fortunately I grew out of it.
   (Which is a spot of sarcasm! It is so easy to drop into.)
   — Never write any letter, especially a business letter, when you are worried or upset. You will regret it.
   — Very few business letters need to be more than one page long. Long letters have been encouraged by the use of the dictation machine, which is one of the curses of the modern

office, and which wastes more time than it saves. (Other people's time, struggling through the long and rambling letters.)

The other curse of the modern office is the photostat machine, which we will be coming to shortly . . .

If you do have that much information to impart, then you should not be writing a letter, but a report. With a short brief letter to accompany it.

How to Write Effective Reports

Traditionally, a report consists of three main parts.

1. The Preamble.
2. The Exposition.
3. The Conclusion.

I have no complaint with the Preamble. It tells what the report is going to be about. I have no complaint with the Exposition. It sets out all the facts and figures that have been gathered in. Clearly set out and edited (in the manner of our 'Ten-point Plan') it should be easy to read. And should end with a summary.

I do have complaint with the usual Conclusion.

'And so we may conclude that the gain in profits on the roundabouts has been negated by the loss on the swings.'

So many reports do just that. They conclude. With quite correct assumptions, no doubt, but in something of a negative manner, with no proposal towards improvement.

■ **A good report ends with some pointer towards useful *change*. That word again!**

Such indication towards change need not be in the form of an appeal, as is usual in a spoken proposal.

— The change could be *already made*:
   '. . . and so I have decided that a Technical Agreement be signed.'
— The change could be *mandatory*:
   'All staff will accordingly follow this new procedure.'
— More usually, the change is *recommended.*
   'It is recommended that this course be followed.'
   (With 'by the Board', or some other indication as to who is to make the decision.)

Most reports divide into one of three 'time' categories.

• Retrospective (what has happened)

• Investigative (what is happening)

• Explorative (what could happen)

Let us look at some examples:

The Sales Report (Retrospective)

One very big advantage to be gained from the writing of a report is that it forces the writer to *think.* You believe that you know all about a subject—until you come to write it down.

Selling people, in my experience, very often need to be taught to think more comprehensively. Selling people tend to work and to think day by day. By asking them to write a monthly (or better, a weekly) report on what they have been doing, they learn to examine their work on a wider basis.

   For this type of report it helps to lay down fixed headings. Our example is for Sales Representatives 'out in the field'.

(i) Results by Personal Turnover.

   The Sales Manager will already know this, and will have thought about this. He wants to be sure that each rep knows and thinks about it too.
      Little calculations should be given to be worked out. (Not

their commission. This they will have worked our for themselves days ago.) But 'Kms travelled per Rand of turnover'
and 'Total face-to-face selling time'. Discovering interesting
indicators like this can make the selling person think deep.

(ii) New Competitive Tactics?

Positive reactions to our products?

Negative reactions to our products?

New Customers?

Customer Activity? etc.

> This information the Sales Manager does not know. So the
> Sales Force is being used as an intelligence network and
> members are being asked to report on matters which they
> observe, but so often neglect to mention.
> (To avoid them going into too many idle words, it should be
> emphasised that it is not necessary to report, each time,
> under every heading.)

(iii) Reasons for low sales.

No problems with comments on this one!

> 'Sales were low last week because I had two punctures. If I
> was given a new car this would not happen.'
> 'Sales were low last week because of my poor territory. If I
> was given a better territory I would do better.'
> 'Sales were low last week because our prices are too high . . .'

Comments, certainly, but not exactly inspiring. So rather ask for
the 'Reasons for High Sales'. And do not accept, 'I sold well last
month because I out-foxed the competition.'

Everybody needs to know *how*.

The Technical Report (Investigative)

The problem with technical reports is that they so easily become
too technical. Non-technical readers do not know what is going on.

■ **At least the Heading and the Summary of any Report should be clear to anybody.**

Non-experts vote the money so that experts can continue!

Scientists working to disciplines tend to become over-obsessed with references and footnotes. The rule seems to be 'Every statement of fact must be meticulously annotated for source'. And the reason given is that by making sure that no unsubstantiated statements creep in, the new work may be quoted as a clean true reference too.

The result of this is that many scientific and quasi-scientific reports end up as being no more than a re-hash of old material. If nothing new has been added, then where is the reason for writing a new report?

■ **A report should report on something that is new. Or should at least offer new views on an old situation.**

A report must give more than facts. There must be new thoughts and opinions and inferences too.

> And it all can be made much clearer if all references can be brought into the body of the work.
>
> Footnotes which have to be looked up at the end are annoying interruptions. Quoting George Bernard Shaw, 'It is like having to go repeatedly to answer the door on your wedding night.' (Readers do not mind a little light relief like this in a dry report. In fact they welcome it.)

The Forward Plan Report (Exploratory)

This type of report looks forward into the unknown so it cannot contain facts. It usually considers the probable results of alternative sets of likely circumstances on a 'What if?' basis.

Many financial investigations fall into this category. They project the probable effects upon hard cash in hand which could flow from various non-financial happenings.

Non-accountants do not always understand this forecasting function of accountants . . .

> Factory Manager: 'I make the goods. The firm would close without me. You numbers people merely write down what I do.'

> Sales Manager: 'Me too. I also am important. I sell the goods. I bring in the money. You do no more than add up my figures.

> Accountant: 'Ah, but I am the one who looks into the future . . .'

Which is why so many Accountants become Managing Directors. They tend to look forwards instead of sideways and backwards, although there is no good reason why exploring the future should be their exclusive domain.

Three quick tips on the writing of a report:

1. Gather all material before you come to any 'Conclusion', or 'Summary', or 'Recommendation'. The answer might not turn out to be as you expected it to be. You are not writing a report to 'Prove something your way'—as can sometimes happen— but to investigate, search, sift, and think, and finally to reach a verdict on the evidence.

2. Do offer a brief overall look on page one.(Sometimes known as the 'Bird's eye view'.)

■ **What this is about**
■ **Main discovery**
■ **What should happen next**

This is so that the busy Big Boss can gather in the main message in one quick glance. (Yes, you do have to write out the complete substance. So that he can pass it along with a 'Here, check this.')
3. Neatness does count. In an ideal world all reports would be neatly typed and neatly bound.

Technical Data Sheets and Instruction Leaflets

These very often seem to become crossed over. The Instruction Leaflet, full of figures, is too technical. The Technical Data Sheet, written in too basic a style, is too brief.

The fault often lies in some specialist being allowed to work away alone. Everything to be printed needs to be at least double-checked.

Secret Revealed!

I hesitated before including the following, a means for generating 'instant descriptions about anything'. It could be mis-used.

Suppose you are sitting before a huge pile of 'Employee Progress Sheets' to which you now have to add your personal comments. You cannot put 'Tries hard and should do well', or similar, on every one, as is done on school reports.

You want to sound a little more original, to show that you have actually thought about each person.

This is how it is done.

Instant Description Generator—Personnel Patting Version

Positive	Praiseworthy	Outlook
Forward-looking	Exemplary	Approach
Strong	Admirable	Manner
Energetic	Useful	Understanding
Realistic	Healthy	Style

Method:

Take any one word from each column in turn and put them all together.

Example:
'Joe Soap has a *positive useful approach.*'
Easy, isn't it?
The frightening thing is that it all works. These phrases, picked at random, sound to be so *profound.*

Take this seriously, or not.
Similar tables could be worked out and used, perhaps *are* being used:

> For padding out reports.
> For lovely-sounding CV's.
> In advertising.

As I say, frightening. It shows how powerful words can be in their meaning and effect upon the reader, even though the writer may have *put no thought to their selection*!

The One Best Word

You have the opportunity *to* think as you write, to *choose* that one best word. For there is always one word, and often one word alone, which will convey the *exact* meaning you intend.

Leave Well Alone

There are some words and phrases which you should avoid, usually because they have drifted into general use without having any definite purpose or meaning.
— Two Latin orphans
    're' as in heading 're Late Deliveries' is superfluous
    'per' as in 'as per your letter' is superfluous
— to 'ise' is not wise
    Capitalise . . . Conceptualise . . . Pragmatise . . .
    There are so many of these synthetics, and all so clumsy. Most have good simple alternatives.
    To maximise the profits . . .

To increase the profits . . .

Which has the greater punch?

— By and large it would seem to me that without further ado we should bring this to a state of conclusion.

Let's stop now.

Slang

Purists of the English language go bananas over the use of slang.

There is not much they can do about it . . .

All languages are alive, they grow constantly, they alter in form. The slang of today will be the accepted speech of tomorrow.

But in the meantime:

- Go easy on the use of the very latest slang in speech.

- Go very easy on the use of any slang in writing.

The Ubiquitous Word Processor

That is a good and suitable word—ubiquitous. It means 'being present and in power all over'. Which describes the wp exactly. Either found alone, or as one of the facilities of the Personal Computer now set beside almost every desk, the wp is firmly established.

Be careful in the use of abbreviations. It is likely that you will read word processor there for wp, particularly as it has just been mentioned in the heading. But some abbreviations are less obvious.

A common failing is the use of in-house abbreviations, such as rog or DDM—which mean nothing at all to those outside, and they are not always all that clear to those inside, either.

Modern usage is for stops to be omitted from abbreviations where possible. OK?

The word processor is a wonderful tool for handling and controlling wads of words, but it can no more guarantee good writing, than can a state-of-the-art camera ensure good pictures.

Always bear in mind that it is your *message* that counts. Your final communication in your final set of words. This is what people will see in print, or perhaps at their terminals, and they will react to what is conveyed. They will not care a jot about how difficult, or how easy, it may have been for you to put the words together.

And the wp is easy to use, ask all those happy devotees who proclaim, 'Don't know how I ever managed without one.'

The keyboard is light and smooth, learning to touch-type is a dream, it is all so simple . . .

Except for wading through the instruction manual . . . Why are so many of these so confused, complex, and obscure? The very worst advertisement for an advance that can lead to clear and polished writing!

To be fair, they have so much to tell. Each new version has so very much extra to offer, so many wonderful features, most of which the average user will never need.

Quick guide to the most efficient use of your wp

1. Study and understand those features that you will use every day.
2. Learn the access for these so well that you never need to call up 'help' nor consult the book.
3. Remain aware that the more involved procedures are available if required.
4. Practise strict discipline, particularly in the saving of files.
    — Back up at regular intervals to avoid loss of work due to hiccups in the power supply. (We all learn this the hard way!)
    — Take an extra back-up of important pieces, just in case the first back-up corrupts. This can happen.

— Establish a logical system for file names.

'What is on this?'
'Where did I put that?'
'How can I find the other?'

All such muddles, and they can be time-wasting muddles, can be avoided.

Once again, for all its wonder and convenience, the wp is no more than a *means*. It is a marvellous device for assembling, sorting, and storing words, but it cannot think.

You still need to work out your message. What it is that you wish to convey.

Spelling

Being able to spell is a gift, like being able to whistle through two fingers. You can either spell or you can't.

If spelling is a problem, then you will need to refer to a dictionery (and that should be diction*a*ry) constantly. Note those words that keep tripping you, and make an effort to memorise their correct form.

For us all, the wp fitted with a spelling checker can be a great boon. Although, and apart, in many versions, from laboring thru American spelling, it can slip up.

Sometimes inexplicably, sometimes explicably . . .

For example:

There chips do not realise that their can be this problem.

> 'There' and 'their' are homonyms. They sound the same but are differently spelled and have different meanings. I'm showing off here, of course. It is so easy to show off by producing obscure words, or specialised words, or obsolete words, to the confusion of everybody.

Punctuation

Some common problem areas:

— Capitals

'Main Street in our karoo town really is a main street and the bank on the corner is the Karoo Town Bank'.

This is to the general convention. Capitals are used when the word is specific, otherwise not.

I tend to use capitals for Emphasis, where capitals should not properly be used. You may have noticed this. But I see no harm, and nor do I see harm in commencing a sentence with 'But'. I write to put my message across, not to win prizes for English literature.

The Rules of Punctuation are more rules to be broken . . .

— Brackets

Brackets are useful when you want to bring a sideways thought into the main message. (As you often do.) They are best used around a separate sentence. Used inside of a sentence, brackets can derail the train of thought, especially if the information introduced (and neat writing is important too) has no direct connection with the subject in hand.

— Quotation Marks

The modern tendency is toward the use of single quote marks rather than double, that is, not only for 'inserts' like this, where their use is normal, but for quoted dialogue too.

OK, so you are not writing a novel, but a business letter or a report. You may still need to quote words exactly as said, in fact you should, for this is stronger.

not . . . He said that he would never agree to this move.

but . . . He said, "I will not agree to this move. Never."

Strictly speaking I am not quite correct there. Dialogue is written down as in the second example. While the reporting of speech, which is what we are doing here, should end . . . Never''. rather than . . . Never.'' With the quotation closing before the full stop.

However, the proper version 'looks wrong' especially to journalists and printers, and this is one of the preferred exceptions shown in most Style Sheets.

These are the guides issued by publishers and newspapers to their staffs to ensure consistency in style. They are very useful to all who have to write . . . articles, technical notes, reports, business letters, or whatever.

■ **Beg, borrow, or steal a Style Sheet if you can.**
■ **Preferably not the latter.**

Memos

FROM THE OFFICE OF P.J. TURNBULL
The use of Company telephones for the purpose of private conversations will cease forthwith.

Very poor example of staff relations. Guaranteed to upset everybody.

Memos are not for the promulgation of imperious commands. Although this is often the way they are used, which has given the memo a bad name.

Memo is short for memorandum, which the dictionary defines as: A note to help the memory. A record of events for future use.

'Help the memory'—as a reminder. This is the purpose for which the memo should be used.

Memo to self: 'Buy new flea collar for dog.'
Memo to staff: 'Don't forget that all Job Reports are due on Tuesday.'

These are for action, but not standing in isolation or appearing out of the blue. They are *reminders* of actions that are already known.

- **A memo is short.**
- **A memo makes one statement.**
- **A memo cannot be used to tell a full story.**

A memo should not be used to *institute* some action which the recipient does not know about.

> 'I have decided that you should take your leave in August.'

A memo should be used to *confirm* an action, already discussed and agreed upon.

> 'At our meeting today you agreed to amend the budget figures before the last day of the month.'

Found stuck to my steering wheel after a minor service.

> MEMO: We have fitted a new manual over-ride to your automatic choke.

They never discussed this with me! They never phoned! They never explained . . . So what's this they've done then? Why? What for? How much will it cost?

If anything is choking, it is me.

This is not the way it should be done. But it is the way it often *is* done. Telling, not reminding.

Other useless memos:

> 'We confirm that the matter is receiving our attention.' (What matter? Attended to by when?)

> 'Please respond to our memo of 31st inst.' (About what? Now I have to look it up.)

Such memos tell nothing useful at all.

Copies to Everyone . . .

I mentioned the photostat machine as being one of the curses of the modern office. It is too easy to keep the thing spinning, sending out a copy to everybody. (This out-of-control unread confetti is known as 'Keeping them all in the picture'.)

'I confirm that you are to shred all last month's letters.'
The particular letters concerned, deal with the personal problems of employees. They are to be destroyed. The Personnel Manager, to whom this memo was addressed, knows this. The staff of the Personnel Department, who were all sent automatic copies, do not.

So all last month's correspondence was destroyed. (This is not a joke example. It is based upon an actual disaster.)

☆ Make sure that the master copy of a memo says
   'For action by . . .'

☆ Make sure that all other copies read 'FOR INFORMATION ONLY'.

Or you will have your own disasters . . .

Put it in Writing . . .

There are people who make the most wonderful promises—verbally.

There are people who have the most terrible memories—invariably.

Reminder memos are very useful—indeed essential—in dealings with such people.

In severe cases you may even need to stand over them while they sign as having 'seen and noted'.

Please respond to My . . .

Another true story.

I once worked for an organisation which had a Financial Director who had a Super Efficient Secretary. She used to deluge me with reminders.

'Please may we have the Sales Forecast promised for the 1st April.'

I phoned her boss. 'Look, I have given you all the figures you need.'

'Yes, I know. Thank you.'

The following week, another memo:

'Please may we have the Sales Forecast promised for the 1st April. This is a second reminder.'

He was getting figures, but he wasn't telling *she*. And so the matter remained open.

'Please may we have the Sales Forecast promised for the 1st April. This is a third reminder.'

Eventually, I phoned the man. 'Look, about all these reminders that your secretary sends out . . .' And he knew nothing at all about it. Miss Super Efficient had started this proliferating reminder system all on her own.

There may be one in your office . . .

Memos, properly and sensibly used, can ease the wheels of Commerce and of Industry.

Memos, improperly used, can be a pain.

★ **Realization!**

> **To write effectively means hard work.**
> **But it can be to my advantage.**

SUMMARY: The Ten Key Points of Chapter 9

1. *Ease* the task of writing by *understanding* the needs of those you write to.
2. Use the *advantages* of the written word. (Polished message, wide audience.)
3. Respect the *disadvantages* of the written word. (One-way message to unknowns.)
4. The written word and the spoken word can be *complementary*. Ideally, *support* the one with the other.
5. Write all business letters as *person* to *person*. Be *courteous*, *straightforward*, and *clear*.

6. A report should *investigate.*
   A report should *point towards useful change.*
7. Use the *best word* for your intended meaning.
8. Be sure of *spelling* and *punctuation.*
9. Use a memo to *remind* of agreed action.
10. Do not *proliferate paper*!

EXERCISES

1. Write a letter to a friend, somebody you should have written to ages ago. Open your heart. Tell of the most exciting thing to have happened to you since you last wrote. Share. Write about him or her too. And do post the letter.
2. Prepare, consider, and write a report on:
   'Ways in which I can improve my work efficiency'
   This is an 'Explorative' report. You are seeking to discover opportunities for useful future change.
   This is also a 'Recommendation' report. You will be recommending to yourself that you follow your own advice.

Not quite so easy, is it?

**When we have to write about a subject,
we suddenly realize:
We have to think to write.**

10

Bring it all together

And so we arrive at the final chapter. This is the end of the book, the conclusion of the course, but the start of all the benefits which you can gain from the application of the full set of skills of 'Effective Communication'.

The time has come to bring together all the elements of the course, to make of them a complete and coherent whole. To summarise all we have discussed into one neat package.

It is also Question Time, the time for feedback. Each year as I complete a course, students ask questions, and on the same recurrent theme—'How will this work for me?'

You may well have the same concern.

'Can I be sure of getting through to people?'
'Will I find the time to try all this?'
'Is this the only way to succeed?'

Before I set out my replies, this is a good place to mention the answering of questions in general. Questions can be traps. Governments have fallen through the careless answering of questions.

Beware the First Question!

You have spoken very well. You know it. Your message went over perfectly. 'Any questions?' you ask. Big smile. 'Yes?'

The first person to jump up is likely to be a repressed extrovert! All frustrated. Bottled up inside. *You* have been speaking. Extrovert has been forced to sit silent.

This first question is likely to be not a question at all, but a lengthy airing of some personal belief.

Hold up both hands. Stop the flow. Say, 'Thank you so much for your point of view. Next.' If this does not work start a handclap.

Awkward Questions

— You do not have to answer awkward questions . . .

'Will we be getting a bonus this year?'

'That is not yet finally decided.'

— You do not have to answer in public . . .

'What about my study leave?'

'May I see you about that afterwards?'

Curb your Quick Wit

Student: 'I am keen to learn how to improve myself in my personal relationships. How can I make a bigger impression on my girl friend?'

Me (quick of wit that day, but slow of wisdom): 'Jump down on her from the top of the wardrobe.'

Never go for a cheap laugh.

You can make an enemy for life.

People will become afraid to ask you anything.

(And I didn't answer the man's question, anyway.)

Do not Invite Trouble

'Go on. Feel free. Ask me anything at all.'

I once worked for a family firm where the Grandfather would gather us all together, periodically, in our own time, for one-sherry-per-person, and a pep talk. 'We are all one big happy family,' said he on one occasion, 'Now would any-body like to ask me a question? Anything at all?

'Yes,' called a voice from the back, 'Why was your son-

in-law made Sales Manager?'
That was the last free sherry we had.

First Recurrent Question

'Can I be *sure* of getting through to people?'
No of course you can't. Nothing is sure in this world, nothing is
ever certain. *But if you do things right* you can improve your odds.

Firstly, *are* you doing it right?
— Do you say what you have to say, clearly, and with a purpose?
— Do you offer some real benefit to your listeners?
— Are you confident, enthusiastic, and sincere?
— Do you smile?
I have had students tell me, 'Yes, cross my heart, I am doing all
that. But people still ignore me . . . .' I believe them. You can do it
all right. You can really really try. And miss the connection.

The Verbal Connection

In order to 'get through' to people you have to add something of
yourself. You have to be *considerate*.
— Am I considering their needs?
— Am I considering their feelings?
— Am I considering all possible effects of my words?

A good Resolution:

> I will consider my words. I will consider their effect upon
> others, who are friendly, and who want to help. I will take
> greater care in my manner.

When you genuinely try to be friendly, and smile, you will get
through. You will make the Verbal Connection!

'Hey stupid! Are you still there in the bathroom?'
Remember that family are people too!

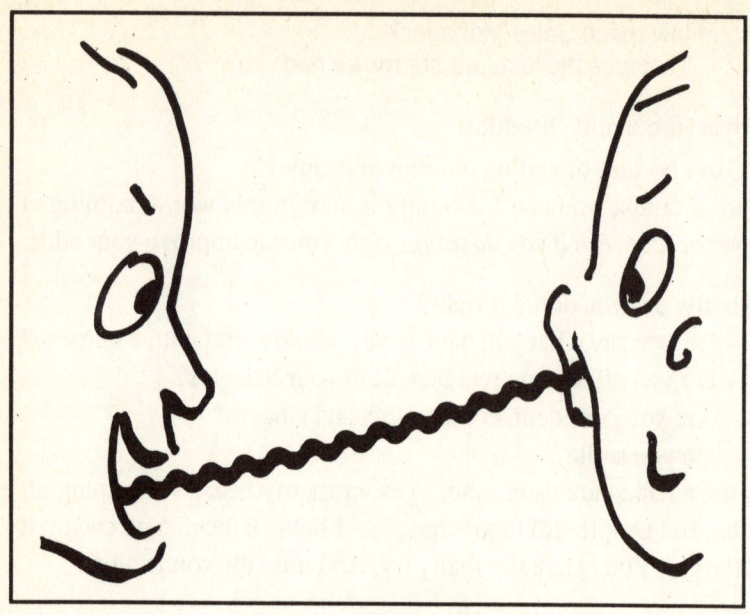

The Verbal Connection

Second Recurrent Question:

'Will I find the *time* to try all this?
— We live in the age of the 'Information Explosion'. There is just too much knowledge about.
— We live in the 'Instant Age'. Instant Food. Instant Information Transfer. Almost Instant Obsolescence . . .
We have to move faster, faster, faster.

> A Japanese visitor to the USA. Host takes him through a hair-raising short cut from the airport. Looks at watch. 'There, I saved you three and a half minutes.'
> 'And what am I going to do with it?'·

We need to be more *sensible* in our use of time. We need to learn to manage our time better. We need to be able to find more time to do more meaningful things.

(Which should not be so very difficult. Most of us do find the
time to watch plenty of unmeaningful TV.)

Life does tend to close in . . . So much to do, so few hours in each
day.

In order to win in the management of your time you have to set
your priorities.

A good question to ask yourself is:

'Will spending time on this now save more time for me later?'

☆ At the start of each day plan out the tasks ahead. This is time
well spent.

☆ Set strategies so that others do not waste your time. This is time
well spent.

☆ Study the skills of 'Effective Communication' for your own
effective use. This is time well spent.

⇨ Should you find yourself in a job where you are given all the
time you need to complete everything and to fiddle and fuss,
then I suggest that you leave. The business is headed downhill.

We will set aside the third of the recurrent questions for the moment
and proceed to:

The Art of the Written Summary

A written summary, a short condensation of a long message, can
be most useful. It does take time to produce a good summary, of
course, but once again this can be time well invested and time well
spent.

■ **A good summary has all the essentials of the full original.**

• Your summary is useful when you come to explain to other
people. Which saves you time.

- Your summary is useful when you come to refresh your memory after an interval. Which saves you time.

A summary can be of your own material—speech, or document, or report. Such a summary is most likely to have been produced by yourself.

A summary can be of the material of others—speech, or document, or report. Such a summary may have been produced by yourself, or by another, not necessarily the originator of the material.

WARNING!

When using any summary by another of material not known to you beware of bias. Use such a summary to inform, never to judge. Judge only from the full original.

The Summary as Validation

A summary need not be of a speech or of a written work. Important discussions often need to be summarised.

Consider this:

You are out on business for your firm. You have concluded a two hour discussion which your client now describes as having been 'Very fruitful.' You settle back, relaxing. He reaches for a pad, 'Now let us summarise what we have discussed and decided.'

You do this, together. You agree on all points, which he sets down as 1 . . . 2 . . . 3 . . .

'Right!' he says, 'I'll get my girl to type this out and run off a couple of copies. Then we will each sign and date as correct and you can take your copy away.'

Back in your own offices, you go over your copy with your immediate boss. 'Very good,' he says, 'Very efficient. We should do something like this.' (He neglects to mention all the wonderful work you put in at the discussion, but this is often the way of things.)

Note: The term 'my girl' for 'my secretary' was quoted a few lines back. People do talk like this but such familiarity shows disrespect, even when used out of earshot. Those in authority can so easily upset members of their staff. The good executive respects, and is respected.

Speciality Summaries

Short as a summary may be, as concise as possible while still being complete, it can still be too long and comprehensive for some people. For them you need to extract a part—the part they are interested in.

That same piece of paper which you brought back—

The Big Boss: 'What's it worth to us, then? What's the bottom line?'
You: 'Twenty thousand rands.'
Which is all he is interested in.

At home: 'How did your big meeting go today?'
'It went well.'
Which is all your family is interested in.

Different Kinds of Summaries

A summary of the same material can be written in quite different ways to suit different viewpoints.

Take, for example, the 'Ten Key Points' which I have been listing at the end of each chapter. They mean something to you, for you will have just read through the preceding material. They would mean far less to somebody who might look at the ends of chapters in isolation, without reading through the book. Taken out and set in a string as a review of 'What this book is about', these reminders would mean very little to prospective readers at all.

So, in order to write a review summary of this book I would need to change my viewpoint. I would have to introduce the most significant content, clearly but briefly, for people to whom it would be entirely new.

Or I could be asked to write a special summary to suit a particular group. Something, perhaps, on 'How this book can be of use to Sales People'. This summary would emphasis the value of those sections which concern selling skills, while not entirely ignoring the remainder of the material.

So:

☆ You can write a *Reminder Summary* to suit those who already know what it is all about. (For yourself. For selected others.)

☆ You can write a *Review Summary* to suit those who do not yet know what it is all about.

☆ You can write a *Speciality Summary* to suit those with a particular interest.

And all from the same material.

Be it in book, speech, report, paper, or article.

Key Points are the Key

How to set about writing a summary of spoken material:

— Use our same skill of asking yourself
  'What is the speaker saying?'
  Which you immediately write down as
  'The speaker is saying that . . .'

— This yields a series of Key Points, from which, adding explanatory detail to suit, you can produce the final summary. You do not need to adhere to the sequence used by the speaker. If you can clarify your summary by revising the sequence, then do so.

How to set about writing a summary of written material:

— *Read it all through first.* More than once, if you feel you need to. You must understand everything very well before you can hope to summarise. This is important.

— Then go through slowly, asking yourself
  'What does the writer mean?'

Which you write down as
'The meaning of this passage is . . . .'
Which again produces the Key Points.

Taking out and examining the *Key Points* of a long message is the secret for producing a meaningful summary.

From the Key Points of any mass of material, spoken or written, your own or from others, you will be able to pummel out and produce your final shining summary. It is hard mental work. You will feel the strain. You will have to continually study and think about the whole of the material.

The Time Cruncher

Wouldn't it be nice if there were an easier way? Can't we set up a computer to do the job for us? Zap zap whirr whirr here we are.

It would seem not. Even using a most elaborate program, with complex tests and decision making, this could be no more than a cutting down of words. Taking out all the a's and the's perhaps, but not capable of finding and extracting the short meaning of a long message.

But there is a way to shorten speech.

There is a machine called a 'Time Cruncher', which looks like a small tape recorder. Set this up, tape a one hour hunk of talk, and then play it back. The playback takes only thirty minutes, and with no Donald Duck voice either. The device works by chopping the sound into lots of little bits, and then using only each second snippet.

I would like to have one of these machines. In fact, I would like to have two. I would like to bring one of my lectures down to thirty minutes, and then play it over, Time Cruncher to Time Cruncher, to bring it down to fifteen. And then again—and again. Crunching the words, shorter and shorter.

What would we end up with, I wonder? A single 'E-e-r-g-h? A grunt?

And a grunt, you will remember, was used in the introduction of this book as a symbol of the non-communicator.

We can summarise *too* far.

'What is Romeo and Juliet about, then?'
'Love.'

And so it is, but there is drama and poetry too.

PROFIT AS YOU PRACTISE TOTAL COMMUNICATION

A Reminder Summary

Before we come to the third and final recurrent question that is asked of me, I offer you a summary of this complete book. This is a reminder summary, the material is already known to you. I have added nothing new.

I suggest that you go carefully through this summary, as a check that you do know and understand all of the skills and implications of 'Effective Communication'.

But knowing, and even understanding, is not enough.

■ **You must use and apply all the skills taught by this course, each and every day.**

Or you will miss your main benefit.

Which is to profit. To be a winner.

From Chapter 1: CALL FOR A CHANGE

Whenever you speak:

HEADLINE what you intend to talk about.   (Tell them the subject)

Explain the **BENEFIT**. (Tell them what they can gain by listening.)

Each time you speak call for some **CHANGE**.

This can be:

Change in **LEVEL OF KNOWLEDGE** (fairly easy . . .)
Change in **ATTITUDE** (more difficult . . .)
Change in **BEHAVIOUR** and **COURSE OF ACTION** (hardest of all, but the one which gets things done.)

The change you call for must:

BENEFIT you   (or why ask?)
BENEFIT them (or why should they change?)
be **POSSIBLE** (or it won't happen)

— Always consider your 'Audience'. (May be only one person.)
— Be sure of your **PURPOSE**. (What are you trying to do?)

From Chapter 2: SPEAK UP WITH CONFIDENCE

Three essentials for confidence when speaking:

Controlled **EXCITEMENT** (Show your **ENTHUSIASM**)
Mastery of **TECHNIQUE** (Know that you have it right)
EXPERIENCE (From Practice, Practice, Practice)

Also:
☆ Talk about *people* rather than about things.
☆ Say what you have to say—in the way that the audience likes to hear.
☆ **SMILE**

And:

Know your First Sentence off by heart
Know your Last Sentence off by heart

Use your **VOICE**

Pitch up and down
Pace s-l-o-w-l-y
Pause frequently

Practise turning your *thoughts* into *words*.

From Chapter 3: PREPARE WITH CARE

Apply the 'Ten-Point-Plan'
1. Headline
2. Break any tension (*short* joke)
3. Explain benefit
4-8 Three to Five **STRONG** points (the first can be a **BLOCK-BUSTER** to gain attention)
9. Sum up
10. Appeal for the change you propose (with an **ARM-TWISTER**—the offer they cannot refuse)

And:

THINK about the effect of your opening.
Make sure that you do Relax your audience (and yourself)
Break l-o-n-g sessions into short Modules.

From Chapter 4: LEARN TO LISTEN

☆ Remind yourself of what you can gain from the speaker.
☆ Discipline yourself to pay full attention.
☆ *You* lose out if you allow your mind to wander.
   Continually ask yourself:
   'What is the speaker saying?'
   Answer in your own words:
   'The speaker is saying that. . . .'
☆ Practice 'Active' listening. Question to understand.
☆ Be a Class One listener! Think beyond the words of the speaker.
☆ Be a 'Listener's Speaker'. Help your audience!

Input from books:

Read with discretion. Be selective. Discuss what you read.

Telephone Tyranny:

Break Free! Use the telephone to *Your* advantage.

From Chapter 5: PERSUADE PEOPLE YOUR WAY

You are in the 'Change Business' of changing others to
— THINK your way
— ACCEPT your way
— ACT your way.
And it is all done by PERSUASION.

To persuade people to change, to your way, point out the BENE-
FITS. To them, from making the change.

Work on the 'Questing Minds'. No need to waste much time on 'Closed Minds'. Nor on those so 'Open' that they sway with every suggestion. (Their conversion is easy, but not permanent.)

(Should your one-person audience be temporarily closed then come back another time.)

Remember that others are always trying to persuade *you*!

☆ Maintain a 'Questing Mind'.

☆ Examine the value, to you, of all proferred benefits, before you commit yourself.

From Chapter 6: ARGUE TO WIN

When persuasion fails you will have to argue. Objections raised must be cleared away by argument before persuasion can continue.

Fend off Aggressive argument. (And never start it yourself.) The Proposal of your Reasoned argument—or Counter-argument—mut be Positive, Clear, and Free of prejudice.

Remember that Logical Reasoned Argument is a contest. *Prove* your proposal. *Disprove* points raised against.

In Negotiation, be sure of the value to you of trade-offs, consider alternatives and compromises, and communicate clearly.

From Chapter 7: USE MORE THAN WORDS

Apart from the words you use, you are judged on:

— Your 'Authority' (Who you are—by past reputation and credibility)

— What you look like (Your appearance must be appropriate)

— How you speak (Watch your grammar and don't let your accent slip)

Basic Body Language:

Be confident and you will look confident. Watch for signs of audience boredom.

Audio Visual Aids:
Use *suitable* aids for the *support* which they can give.

From Chapter 8:GAIN FROM MEETINGS AND INTERVIEWS

CONSIDER other people. Each is quite different from yourself.

In *Conversations*, you must speak up to be noticed.
In *Discussions*, do not be a passenger. Participate, or your views and interests cannot be known.
In *Committees*, common-sense can accomplish far more than conformity to custom. (When Chairing, you need to be **PILOT, REFEREE,** and **ACTIVATOR**.)
In an *Interview*, the Questions are important, but the answers transfer the information. Use questions to lead, probe, and define.

From Chapter 9: EFFECTIVE WRITING

Good writing requires hard work. But good writing does produce results.

Your *Business Letters* should be written as person to person.
Your *Reports* should introduce the subject, investigate the matter, present the facts, and then recommend a useful change.
Your *Memos* are best used as short reminders.

From Chapter 10: BRING IT ALL TOGETHER

— Watch out for Questions! They can trip you.
— Get through to people! Make a Verbal Connection.
— Spend time on improving your level of Communication! This is time well spent.
— Make and use Summaries! Like this one.

The Final Answer

Now, finally, to that third question often asked of me:

'Is this the only way to succeed?'

Which is often enlarged upon:

'I do not agree with all the methods that you teach. What if I use some of my own ideas instead? Would they work?'

My reply:

'Provided that your ideas are sensible, and applied with confidence and enthusiasm, there is no reason why they should not work.

'Provided that you have developed a basic *feeling* for communication you will succeed. You will profit from all your dealings with others. And these benefits will continue, for long after this course has ended.'

Or this book has been read.

Student: 'So what you are saying is that all this detail which you teach so dogmatically is not so critical after all.'

Me: 'No. And I am emphatic, I hope, rather than dogmatic. Each technique which I teach is important. I have tried and tested every one. I have taught them to very many who have also found them to work.'

Student: 'But you just said we can make up our own stuff . . .'

Me: 'Mine is not a full set, not the total answer to all your needs in communication. You will require other specialised and personal techniques, which you will need to develop for yourselves.'

That is why, in the lecture course, and in this book, I encourage people to think through, to understand, to know the reasons why.

You may need to ask a favour of somebody . . . There is nothing directly in these pages on 'How to ask a favour'. But by using the principles you have learned and by applying that most valuable of assets—common-sense—you will be able to work out your own effective procedure.

☆ Have I this feeling for communication?

☆ Can I reason through?

This is your final test. The true examination.

★ The Overall Realization!

I benefit by:
Participation
Showing my enthusiasm
Listening to the real message
Bringing about change
Being total **ME**

The Continuing EXERCISE

There is no benefit to be had in merely thinking about things.

So:

Practise Effective speaking

Practise Effective listening

Practise Effective writing

Use all you have learned

Today and every day.

And Profit . . .

This is not 'The End'.